STORIES OF INDIA

STORIES OF INDIA

Moral, Mystical
Spiritual and Romantic

By

ROSE REINHARDT ANTHON

GYAN

Published by

Gyan Publishing House
5, Ansari Road
Daryaganj, New Delhi-110002
Phone: 011-47034999, 9811692060
E-mail: books@gyanbooks.com

Distribution Network
gyanbooks.com
India, USA, Canada, UK, Australia, France

ISBN : 978-81-212-6290-3 (PB)
First Published, 1906

2nd Impression 2022

Printed at: Gyan Press, Delhi.

STORIES OF INDIA
Author: ROSE REINHARDT ANTHON

STORIES OF INDIA

Moral, Mystical
Spiritual and Romantic

BY

ROSE REINHARDT ANTHON

1906

TO

THE DEAR MEMORY

OF

MY MOTHER

ELIZABETH R. ANTHON

I DEDICATE

THESE LEAVES OF HINDOO LORE

THE GIFT OF MY GOOROO

PREFACE.

The outlines of these Stories of India came to me from one of the most authoritative teachers of Hindoo wisdom. To me they were fraught with deep interest as they gave me an insight into the old Hindoo custom of imparting knowledge and an understanding of many things that before had seemed mere superstitions to me.

So I dress them in garments of my own poor weaving and send them forth into the Western world with the hope that though they lack much of the color and beauty of their original dressing, yet they may inspire in others the interest they have awakened in me.

THE AUTHOR.

New York, 1906.

CONTENTS

The Singer and His Teacher........ 9
The Straight Path........ 18
The Magic Casket........ 22
The Saint and the Snake........ 28
The Yogi and the Housewife........ 33
The Emperor and the Sage........ 41
The Hermit and the Householder........ 45
All for the Gooroo's Books........ 55
The Yogi and the Hunter........ 61
Real Renunciation........ 68
The Hermit and the Villager........ 73
Matching the Pearl........ 79
The Oak and the Vine........ 109
The Moon-Maiden........ 114

STORIES OF INDIA

THE SINGER AND HIS TEACHER

The golden voice of the court-singer rose fuller and richer, filling every corner of the great hall, rolling wide into the corridors and forcing its limpid sweetness into the innermost heart of the Palace where the Empress and her maidens sat in enraptured silence, with swelling hearts and deep-drawn breath listening to him, the world-famed singer, whose voice was drawn from Heaven and who drew toward Heaven all who listened to that Heavenborn voice.

"Oh!" said the Empress, "surely that voice speaks to my heart of the land of my fathers, and again I hear the fountain-splash as I play with my sisters and brothers in the cool of the evening and weave the garland to throw about the beloved form of the Goddess who would bless me with a lord, faithful and true, even as is my own dear lord."

"And to me, fair Queen," said a pensive maid, "he sings of the sister that was my playmate and who was dear beyond words to me, but who, in her early youth, grew very tired of much play and would lie gazing on the shadows that the turrets threw upon the courtyard floor for hours and hours until at last it seemed they wanted her even more than we did. And one day I came upon her and she lay so still and gray as if she had partaken of the last long evening shadow, and when I touched her, she did not stir nor look at me. When my father came, he said to me, taking her in his arms so tenderly, 'Alas, little one! She hath gone out of the shadow into the sunlight that is for such as she!' "

And the littlest maid of honor broke the sad silence and said, "His voice, O Queen, makes me think of the dawn before the dew is dry on the roses, when the birds are greeting each other, and the fawns skip and jump in the moist gardens and the black night has given way to the first golden smile of the sun. It is then I want to go forth and speak to all the living things that are so wide awake, and greet them, even as they greet the coming day. And when his voice bursts forth so glad and happy then, O Queen, I feel the early morn is with me and all the world rejoice in living and all the living rejoice in the world."

"O Queen, thou kindly one! When I hear his voice," said yet another companion of the Empress, "it is as if I were in the House of the Great God again, making offerings for the son that I wanted so much and was not born to me, or as if I sat again in the silence of the night and waited for the footsteps of him, my lord, who was my all on earth and now my all in glory."

And the sweet-faced widow turned away her eyes, wide-gazing into the distance, while in the audience chamber, the Singer, whose wonderful voice had roused memories sad, sweet and glad, in the hearts of the hearers of the inner chambers, stood smiling before the Emperor who showered upon him praises and gifts because of the joy his song had given him. Akbár the Great, the Grand Mogul, Emperor of all that realm, he, the wise and just and learned King, had taken into his court Tánsen the Singer, and unto his heart, Tánsen the Man. Of all his courtiers and subjects, Tánsen was to him the dearest and best friend. It mattered not how wearied was his body, how tired his brain, how sad his heart or how troubled his spirit, the voice of Tánsen ever soothed him into restfulness—the golden voice that filled the heavens with its beauty, that pierced the god-realms with its sweetness, that stormed the thunders with its strength, that cleft the clouds by its plaintive sadness. This was the magic voice that now thrilled through the heart of the King banishing every discord and crowning him with a peace and contentment that rarely sits upon the brow of King or nestles in the heart of man.

"O, Tánsen," said the Emperor, "tell me wherefrom came this voice of yours, whence the wonder of it? It is not of mortals, but of the gods. No other voice such as thine blesses the ear of man, my friend, and gladly would I listen for aye to its marvel."

"You are kind, O Sire," the Singer replied, "but could you hear the voice of him who taught me, whose beauty of voice I reflect so little, could you but hear him, all my poor efforts would be forgotten."

"Ever is your answer thus, O Tánsen! But tell me who is he, this wonderful gooroo of wonderful voice?"

"He is but a hermit, Sire, a saint who lives in the jungle of Brindában. By all he is known as a holy man and his voice hath the power of drawing all unto himself. Will not your majesty go with me on a pilgrimage to the holy forest where you may hear for yourself this voice of wonder and forget that Tánsen ever knew how to sing?"

"No, my friend, yours is unjust humility. To forget your golden voice is impossible, for there is none like it. But gladly will I go with you to this hermit, your Gooroo, to prove what I already know that you are the greatest singer of the world. Let all be made ready for our journey tomorrow."

So the next day as the Emperor, disguised and seated on a huge elephant, started on a pilgrimage with Tánsen to the latter's Gooroo, he said to the singer, "Tell me, O Tánsen, how met you the Saint-Singer and how became you his chelá?"

"It is quickly told, your majesty, it may interest you. My father was a Brahman living in the outskirts of a jungle. We were very poor and I was his only child. Often the passersby from the jungle would stop at our little fruit grove and strip from the trees the fruits that meant the livelihood of our family. One day my father said to me, 'Tánsen, my son, do you watch this side of the grove and call to those wayfarers that seek to steal from our trees.' So I sat within our little raised watch shed and while there I remembered how I had, one terrible day, heard the roar of a stricken tigress as she neared the village in search of her stolen cubs, and day after day I tried to give that roar until it became so perfect that my father fled from the grove on one occasion as he heard it, thinking a tiger was upon his land. After that our fruits were safe, for, as soon as I heard any one approaching with intent to steal, I gave the roar, and instantly they were lost to view in the distance.

"'One evening, as I sat in the watch-cot, I saw through the trees a band of men coming toward the grove. I gave my roar and all, save one, fled. But the one made straight toward me, looking not at me, but into the undergrowths. I shall never forget the love in his face. It seemed that it must draw me down from the cot, and I understood only then the stories I had heard of these holy men, who feared neither man nor beast, and how, by their love the taint of the world was banished from the hearts of the men they looked upon, and the lust of blood quelled in the breasts of the savage beast. The saint struck at the thickets with his staff to look for the tiger, then turned and looked at me lying in my shed, and said: 'What are you doing there, my little man? Have you no fear of the tiger that seems to be lurking near here?' 'Oh no,' I answered, 'I am here to guard my father's fruit grove from the bold thieves that stripped them. There is no tiger here, sir, I roar at them and they think it is a tiger and flee from here. And so my father's trees are safe.'

"'Smilingly he lifted me down from the cot and hoisting me upon his shoulders, walked toward the house where he sojourned for the night much to the joy of my father and mother who felt themselves blessed by his presence within their lowly abode. The next day he left and I with him. He had seen possibilities in the voice of the child that could easily imitate the roar of a tiger, and had promised my father the reward of a world-famous singer for the sacrifice of his son. So I lived with him and loved him, this great Saint-Singer Hari Dás, until you, O Sire, heard my poor voice and took me to your court and home, and most of all, to your mighty heart."

Two days later, as the sun threw its rays athwart the hillside, the King and singer found themselves at their journey's end, and Brindában, holiest ground in all India, lay before them—Brindában, sweetest word of Indian tongue, most sacred spot where Krishna walked and talked, and where lovers of Him still walk that they may partake of the glory that His Blessed Feet have left on its hallowed dust.

There, in this forest of Brindában, before a small hut, they beheld a man sitting in deep meditation, hands folded on breast, head lifted high, eyes closed, and on his brow the glow like the sun's first waking.

"See, it is he, my Gooroo the Saint-Singer," whispered Tánsen, reverently. "Tarry thou here, O Sire, behind these bushes and I will see how it can be brought about that you shall hear this voice so gloriously beautiful and yet so often silent in the presence of the idly curious. Gold, nor jewels, nor titles can bring it from that golden throat. But the smallest action of love will set it vibrating to the pulse of Nature's heart."

So saying, the singer prostrated himself low before his Gooroo, who, wrapped in meditation, saw him not, nor heard him. Then lifting up his head, Tánsen burst forth in a sacred song which his Gooroo had taught him years ago. Louder and louder rang the tone, sweeter and sweeter grew its beauty until suddenly the golden notes broke and harsh discord jarred on the listening ear. The Saint-Singer opened his eyes and spake.

"Thou art out of key. Thou dost distort the beauty of sound, O Tánsen, thou who wert so perfect, art imperfect and discordant. Thou golden-throated one, has dallying with the court and the world lost for thee the soul of harmony?"

The singer, who purposely had made the harsh discord, said, "O Gooroo! I pray thee, sing thou the strain that I may again bring it to memory."

Then the Gooroo lifted his voice and pealed forth the harmonies of Heaven-sounds. It told of the song of the stars, of the marriage of earth and seas, of the weavings of love that give sustenance to man and all that lives, of the birth of Time and the crowning of Eternity, of the creation of gods and the dance of Love, each step of which is the making of a universe, each circle of which is the immutable law thereof.

And, as he sang, Akbár fell on the ground drunk with the exquisite blessedness of it.

The chelá stood wrapped in devotion before that Saint-Singer, and when the song ceased and its sweetness still throbbed through the silence of the evening, Tánsen's hushed voice fell upon the ear of the holy man, saying, "The Badshah hath come to pay thee homage, O Gooroo."

And when Akbár the Great had fallen at the feet of the humble saint and risen again, he walked a little in the lengthening gloom with his singer and said, "Thou art right, Tánsen. He is all thou sayest. Thou art a shadow, he a sun. Thou art as brass, he is gold. Why is this great difference and what the cause? Both of you have the sound of Heaven in your voice, the gold of harmony in your tones. So like, yet so different."

"The difference, O Sire," answered Tánsen, "is vast as you say, but the cause is simple. I sing to please an earthly King. He sings to please the King of Kings.

THE STRAIGHT PATH

A minister of a great king, seated in his palanquin, was making for the palace, when he saw a man, clad in ill-fitting garments and bearing himself as one of the poorest laborers of the kingdom, digging a pit at the side of the road. The minister called a halt to his carriers and said to the digger of the pit: "Why dost thou dig that pit? Knowest thou not, thou fool, that a danger it is to the passer-by, who seeing it not, may stumble therein?"

The digger replied with a wise shake of his head: "A fool thou callest me; a fool indeed is he who falleth into my pit! For, O sir, he that walketh in the straight path, cannot fall therein, and he who falleth therein is the man that maketh a crooked path; for my pit is on the roadside, and not in the pathway."

The minister, noting the wisdom of the retort, ordered his servants to take the man into his house, to clothe him, feed him, house him until his return. The next morning he called the laborer to him and said: "Thy reply of yesterday hath interested me because of its wisdom. Wilt thou remain in my house and give me more of thy counsel when I shall have need of it?"

And so he that had seemed an ordinary laborer became the counselor of the minister. And so wondrous was the wisdom and the counsels so good he brought to state affairs, that in a short time the minister became Prime Minister of the King.

Now the people of the court began to wonder at the new wisdom of the Minister, for he had ever been known among them as one of not overmuch brightness, but wearing ever on his brow the semblance of wisdom, but not its true image. And they began to pry into his private affairs and look about for the cause of his enlightenment, until one day, by the unfaithfulness of a menial, they learned of the inmate of his house that was ever in close companionship with the Minister, and quick the talking spies acquainted the King of the source of the Minister's wondrous wisdom.

When the Prime Minister heard that the world was about to know how and where he came by his wisdom, a great panic took hold of him, and he forgot all but his desire to rid himself of the man who had been his friend and counselor, but now was his seeming rock ahead. So, after thinking about it all night, he called to him the wise man, who, though he served the Minister at all other times as a menial servant, was in reality one of the greatest sages of his time, who preferred to live unnoticed in the guise of a poor tramp and laborer, happy within himself in the enjoyment of the luxuries of the realm of thought and wisdom. Handing him a letter, he said: "Take thou this letter unto him whose name is written thereon; see that thou thyself doth deliver it into his own hands. A matter of great import it containeth, and life or death dependeth on its delivery."

So spake the Minister; and the sage went forth to deliver the letter to him for whom it was intended.

It chanced that the young son of the Prime Minister encountered the sage on his way, and, with beaming face and lighted eye, he said unto him: "Wilt thou do something for me? My sweetheart awaits me up yonder; my father awaits me at the palace. Wilt thou not take this letter to her, the sweetest lady in all the land, and bring back to me her answer?"

The man looked at the bright, eager face of the youth, then at the letter in his hand, and said: "It cannot be; a commission your father hath sent me on that brooketh no delay. See, yonder is the house; there must I deliver this letter."

The youth looked up and said: "'Tis but a short distance. Give me the letter, and I will deliver it to him who is the state executioner, to whom it is addressed, and do thou go unto her, my mistress, and bring me back a reply within the hour."

A moment the sage paused, then the youth snatched the letter from his hand and put in its place the love letter to his mistress.

An hour later the sage reappeared at the house of the Prime Minister and inquired for the youth.

"What dost thou here?" the Minister asked. "Did I not send thee with a letter to him who would not have sent thee back to me thus?" The sage replied: "Oh, sir, thy son insisted upon my going with a letter to his mistress while he himself took charge of the letter thou gavest me. See, here is an answer from her whom he sent me to."

At this the Prime Minister uttered a wild shriek and, falling on his face, cried: "What have I done? Woe is to me, accursed am I forever and ever! My son is dead, dead! Thou fool, that letter was the death warrant of the person who delivered it unto the executioner to whom it was addressed. My poor son! With thine own hands hast thou delivered thy death sentence."

"O thou greater than fool! Thou hast fallen into my pit," cried the sage. "So long as thou didst walk in the straight path, thou wert safe and prospered, but when thou didst take the crooked road, thou didst fall into the pit."

THE MAGIC CASKET

It was audience day at the court, the day when the rich and poor, the mighty and lowly and all who elected might come to the king in person to present to him their woes and wrongs and appeal to him for succor and aid and pray to him to right their wrongs and lift from them any weight of oppression with which they were overburdened withal.

On his throne sat the king in regal splendour, with his prime-minister at his side, promising succor to each, giving light and cheer to many hearts that erstwhile had been overshadowed.

Now it chanced that a little way from the king a very ragged man stood, gazing past the throne, as if into an undiscovered country beyond. He had evidently forgotten his own surroundings or even the errand upon which he had come, and wrapped in thought he alone of all the supplicants had failed to ask of the king a boon.

Suddenly the king turned to his prime minister and said: "Who is it that takes the best care of the body of a man in this world?"

The prime-minister answered without hesitation: "Why, the wife, of course, your majesty."

"If she be chaste," came in calm, even tones from the lips of the ragged man who stood near the dais; "if she be not chaste, she careth not for him, whether body or soul, and may desire the destruction of even both, your majesty."

The king smiled and turning to his minister said again: "What thing is of most service in this world?"

"Money, your majesty, for with it all things pertaining to the world can be had."

"If it be in the hand," said the ragged one in the same thoughtful manner.

The king, noting the apparent wisdom of both replies, beckoned him to come nearer, and said: "Who art thou, and what dost thou here? Already all supplicants have told me their needs and thou alone remainest here and still hast asked naught of me. What can I do for thee?"

The man answered: "Your majesty, I had not thought ever to come to thee for aid, nor would I, were it not for the sake of one who is dear beyond all the world to me, my wife. A scholar am I, my books have been my wealth, my all. Days and nights I have spent, devouring them to the exclusion of all things else. More cared I for wisdom than worldly goods, O king, nor feared or dreaded I poverty, while I was able to procure food for her, who is most worthy of women, and a little to eat and drink for myself. Thus was my world all bright and beautiful, until yesterday I awoke to the fact that she, my loved one, was nigh illness, because of lack of good food, and to thee I have come to pray for aid, not for charity, O king, but to render thee my service and mayhap be able to supply her with the necessary nourishment, so that she, who is dear to me, may again smile upon me as of yore because of her returning health and strength."

The king looked at the gaunt figure covered with ragged garments, then into the calm, sweet light of his eyes, overshadowed by a brow of height and wisdom, and said unto his minister: "I make him one of the learned men of my court; see that his needs are fully supplied and add unto them such luxuries as befit one of that position."

From that day on the ragged scholar was known all over the land as the most learned man of the court, and though he wandered no more in his rags, he was still poring over his books every leisure moment that was not given to his master. For his gentle manners and kind deeds too, he was noted far and wide, and the wife, who had looked upon him as a god in the days of poverty, now saw in him the saint indeed. For while his position and wealth had brought change in his surroundings, in the student no change had come, but only in the garments he wore.

And so in a short time he was made minister of the court and the king's love for him was great because of the rare counsels which he gave and the beauty of his daily living.

But at court there were those who grew jealous, that he, a ragged beggar, should have reached such heights at court, and many rumors went out with intent to poison the mind and heart of the king toward the minister, and one and another said unto the king again and again: "He is versed in magic, O king, it is known that each day, before he goes to thee, he retires into an inner chamber and opens a silver chest and there bows low to the ground before the charm that is therein. He hath bewitched thee, sire, for it is unnatural that one, who only a year ago came to thee begging in rags, should be so loved by thee and hold a place at court second only to thee. Think of it, O king, and beware of his magic art."

At first the king laughed at his courtiers, but when the warning came to him again and again, even from those nearest to him, he grew a little grave and there arose in his mind a suspicion, ever so slight, against his minister, and one day he said unto them: "Come and I will go with you and see for myself."

So, with his courtiers he proceeded to the house of his friend, the minister, who, in his simple, gracious way, made them welcome in the magnificent home which the king had bestowed upon him. After an exchange of courtesies, the king said unto him: "Come with me at once to my council chamber, for there are weighty matters about which I would consult with thee."

The minister said after a pause: "If thy majesty will permit, may I retire into privacy for a few moments?"

A look of malicious pleasure passed between the courtiers, but the king only said: "I wish thee to come at once."

Again the minister hesitated and said, "'Tis but for a moment I would retire, thy majesty. I beg thee to permit me to do so."

A shadow passed over the face of the king, as he said: "What wouldst thou do?"

"Just for a moment retire into this inner chamber, thy majesty, and I will follow thee to the palace."

The courtiers rubbed their hands in glee and as the king rose and said to him, "I will accompany thee, my friend," the minister, alarmed, drew back.

"Thy majesty, it is not fit for thee to come where I go. It would mean naught to thee, but it is all to me."

Then it is so, thought the king, as he insisted to be taken with the minister, who led him into a little chamber, that was filled with books and pamphlets, and in the center of the room a casket stood. The minister gazed at the king, who, with disapproval in his eyes, gazed back at him. Then without a word, he opened the lid of the silver chest and behold, in the bed of silver lay a bundle of old yellow rags!

''What is it?'' the king asked.

''O, sire! These are the rags which covered me in my days of poverty. I have kept them so that in my days of prosperity I might not forget the man who wore them. Each day before I go to your council chamber, I look upon them and remember what I needed in those days, and what I felt in those rags, so that I may not forget what the poor feel and need.''

The king heard these words in wondering admiration, and leading the minister back to the courtiers, he said unto them in deep scorn: ''Out of the magic chamber I have come, O my friends; upon the magic casket and its charm I have looked, and now I shall pass sentence of punishment upon the magician himself, and proclaim him here Prime Minister of all my realm.''

THE SAINT AND THE SNAKE

Thus it was writ: A saint passing through the forest came to a path across which was stretched in great black length a serpent, who showed not the signs of venomous hatred, as are the serpents wont to do. The saint was known as one of the most holy in the land, and was also looked upon as one of the wisest sages, because of his wondrous fund of wisdom and understanding of the laws of the universe and the voice of Nature itself, the chirp of the bird, the call of the wild beast of the jungle, the rattle and hiss of the serpents themselves. He understood even to the extent of knowing all they meant by their sounds and motions.

Now among holy men there is a law which is never broken, and that is, that over the body of no living, breathing creature of the Lord's making will they step, since all these creatures, even in their lowest state, are worthy to turn aside for. For are they not the beloved creatures of the hand of Him for whose love and beauty the saint had left all to worship and so come closer unto Him for whom alone he now lived?

So, standing close to the serpent, the saint, who by his love knew how to address the serpent, said: "O serpent, across my path thou liest. Wilt thou not move even a little to the side so I may pass? I cannot step over thee, who art created by Him whom I worship, for thou too, some day, mayest walk as I do and worship even as I do."

The serpent reared his head aloft and made answer: "O saint, because of thy coming I am here in thy path. Bid me, O holy man, and I will leave thy path. Tired am I of my creeping, crawling life, and long for higher things. Tell me this, how can I, who have stung to death many a bird and beast and man and even those creeping things of my own family, how can I, even low and poisonous, become better? How can I expiate my sins? How can I cease to be feared and accursed wherever I am seen?"

The saint with a wealth of love in his face said unto him: "Sting no more, O serpent, and the curse shall be lifted from thee."

And the snake made way for the saint to pass. On the side of the path the snake lay in the sunshine with closed eyes and languorous body, when a troop of children passed that way. On seeing the snake they ran wildly away, never turning to the right nor left, until they had reached their homes.

The next day they passed again that way, and to their amazement saw the snake in the same place and in the same position. "It is dead," they thought, and, taking great sticks, they poked the snake, who only writhed with pain, but lifted not its head to strike them. Thus bolder and bolder the children became until, as the days went by and they had pelted the serpent with stones and poked him with sticks to their own contentment and the pain of the serpent, they boldly went to its head, opened its jaws and thrust their hands between them, down into its throat. Still the snake hurt them not, but even opened its mouth to the width of its extent, to keep the poison bag from touching the hand of the cruel little urchins who tortured him thus.

For many days, the lads played and hurt the snake, who, though he suffered much, made no sign nor sought to strike back. One day it so chanced that some wood-cutters passed by that path, and after gathering faggots in great abundance, found they had no cord or rope with which to bind them, and spying the serpent so still in the distance, said: "It must be dead or very old; let us tie up our faggots with it."

And straightway they proceeded to use him as a great rope. In the tying, the poor serpent was stretched and pulled and ripped and cut, yet he made no sign to retaliate or in any way use the venom that was within him. So the men carried their faggots to market on the outskirts of the forest.

Reaching there they threw the bundle on the ground, and, untying the snake, cast him on the wayside, where he lay throbbing, quivering and aching with torturous wounds.

For hours he lay there, then, with a gasp, he lifted his eyes and beheld before him the saint, who had told him to sting no more if he wished to expiate the sins of his past. "O saint," gasped the snake in the bitterness of his pain, "I am the snake whom only a short while ago thou didst behold sleek and smooth and beautiful in my grace and motion. Look at me now, bleeding, tortured and wounded unto death am I, because I stung not those who tortured me, when they beheld me harmless. Wise thou mayest be, O saint, and holy, but thy counsel to me was not of deep wisdom, when thou didst say, 'Bite not,' yet surely He, who made me, meant not that this suffering should be mine."

The saint replied, all the while gazing into the eye of the snake: "Unto thee, O poor sufferer, I did say, 'Bite no creature,' but I did not say, 'Hiss thou not at those who take advantage of thy meekness and thy desire to harm no one.' Thy hiss to thee was given as a harmless and timely warning to those who unworthily would gain advantage over thee. This thou mightest have done and the hiss would have taken the place of a bite, without the danger and the hurt.

"Self-preservation is the law that is of greatest growth in the heart of all creatures, and to thee thy hiss and venom were given to serve as weapons that all men fear. Even now, O snake, look about thee and see those who are ready to add torment to thy already battered and mangled body, because of thy seeming helplessness. At one hiss from thee, they will be scattered and thou wilt be feared, although thou dost not inflict pain. Man hath learned to fly even from the shadow of pain, and thy hiss, though not of real danger, is ever a forerunner of it. Hadst thou done this, beautiful and smooth thou still wouldst be and yet thy expiation also would have been fulfilled."

The snake, after this, lifted up his poor head and gave forth hiss after hiss, and in a few seconds the market place was deserted. He then drew his weakened body after him and crawled into the dark inclosure of foliage and there remained, hissing at those who came close unto him with danger intent, but striking not with the poison that was to him a weapon of sure death to all that it touched.

Thus to great age he advanced, and, though never biting creatures, he held at bay with his hiss those who sought to molest him.

THE YOGI AND THE HOUSEWIFE.

In a small jungle of India, the wayfarers were wont to see sitting in stern and harsh silence a yogi, with hands crossed upon his breast and his eyes closed for hours at a time, while he meditated in deep concentration upon the laws of Nature within the universe and within himself. The good peasants of the neighboring village passed him with bated breath and rarely stopped to look upon him save with eyes of fear, for the lines of love were not stamped upon this yogi's face, nor was he full of that sweet humanity or humility which the holy ones who dwelt in the jungles were apt to display in their silent and ardent quest for illumination.

One day, as the yogi took his accustomed seat 'neath his tree of meditation, he was startled out of his deep trance-like silence by the droppings of a heron that sat on a branch above him. The angry yogi flashed a burning glance at the innocently-offending heron, and lo, at that glance, the heron fell at his feet dead, for the fire in the glance of the angry yogi had taken the life of the bird!

The yogi gazed at the havoc he had wrought on the poor heron, but no pity stirred in his breast for the life he had taken. Only a great throb of conscious power rose within him at this sign of accomplished ambition. "Now," thought he, "I am a real yogi. I may not be able to remove mountains or look at the invisible workings of the universe. I may not be able to put off my body at will or call from a distance a man or a beast in a second. I may not be able to materialize objects for all the world to wonder at. But I can, with a look of anger, slay a life. So, let all beware that they anger me not, lest I show them my power at the cost of their lives." So thought the yogi and again entered into the concentrated silence of meditation.

Now, as the day wore on, he rose and sought the village to ask for the frugal meal that a yogi is wont to beg from the homes of the pious each day. He called aloud at the door of a poor Brahman and demanded in harsh tones for his fare from the lady of the house who opened the door to him. "One moment, Sir," she said, "And I will bring to thee such food as I have," and bowing to the yogi she turned and reentered her house.

The moments passed and lengthened into the half of an hour ere the housewife again came to the yogi, bringing him choice fruits and sweetmeats, and holding them toward him with sweet humility and downcast eyes. But the yogi thrust them away and harshly said, "Ha, 'tis a fine way you treat a holy beggar keeping him waiting at your door to suit your will! Do you know who

I am?" And he cast an angry glance at the woman who met that glance with calm humility and wise serenity.

"Oh yes, Sir," she softly said, "I know who you are. But I am a woman and not a heron whom you can kill by an angry glance."

The yogi started and looked at her in wonderment, but ere he could question her how she came to know of the heron, the Brahmani replied:

"I am a yogi, too, good Sir, and the things that are I see. For me space holds no obstacle and material environments do not cloud my spiritual sense. I read the thoughts of men and that which transpires in the far distance is revealed unto me. So I saw you in anger slay a heron and I read the thoughts in your mind at my long delay in serving you with food, and now again, a moment ago, I knew the desire to punish me swelled in your breast. But, good Sir, your power is lost on me for mine offsets yours. Mine is born of spiritual devotion to duty and kin, while you seek psychic powers for self-aggrandisement. But, pray, pardon my prattle, Sir, I will now tell you how, against my desire, I have kept you waiting thus for these fruits. It is written in the Sacred Books that a woman's first duty is to her husband and home. By this devotion she may gain greater spiritual development than by any other means. You Brahmans teach these and we who read or hear the Shástras in earnest must follow each teaching. So it happened that when I left you, my husband had just returned from a long journey, hungry and almost overcome with weariness and heat. As my first duty is to him, I cooled him, served him and fed him. He is head of our house, the first in my soul and the lord of my heart. Through his great devotion to God, he has been blessed with wonderful illumination of Truth. This illuminated Truth he bestows upon me freely. He feeds me, he clothes me, he keeps the roof-tree above me by his labors. His love comforts me, his strength encourages me, his Truth teaches me and he serves me with his wisdom. And in turn I, most blessed among women, see in him my spiritual guide, my benefactor and my lover. So, with all devotion and humility I serve him and my attention to him is ever undivided. It is through this loving devotion to my good husband, my good Sir, I have attained these spiritual powers which make the invisible visible and the unreadable knowable to me."

The yogi marvelled as he listened to her words. His eyes lost their cold hauteur and the harsh lines softened about his face.

"Thou art indeed a wonderful woman," he said, "and thy words make my heart drop its head in silence because of foolish and harsh vanity. Oh tell me words of advice that might be of service to me in this my quest for illumination, for great is thy wisdom and marvellous thy devotion must be to have brought about this development of soul in thee.''

''Nay,'' said the housewife, ''it is not meet I should teach thee, a Brahman, but this will I say that the same devotion that gave me these spiritual powers show me that thou art an only son of thy parents and in seeking to develop thy soul, thou hast left behind thee, in great pain and sorrow, thy good parents who are pining for thee. There thou hast fled thy highest duty, and because of it, the true light has not been vouchsafed to thee. I urge thee to go yonder across the market place. There thou wilt find a hunter, a man of low caste indeed—a pariah—but of great wisdom. Do thou go to him and ask his advice, and thou shalt hear that which shall make thee wise and see that which thou shalt not soon forget.''

''But,'' said the Brahman, ''a hunter! How can I be in the presence of one who kills living things for a living. An outcast is he and of unclean birth.''

''But thou didst kill a heron, though a Brahman. That wise hunter follows the calling of his caste, Sir, the caste of a hunter in which he is born. But he does not kill, he merely sells flesh as his forefathers did by buying it from somebody else. But even a pariah may acquire wisdom if he desire it, say the sages, wisdom's gate is opened as wide to the meanest born as to the twice-born, even as God is equally approachable to high and low alike. Even from an illuminated Sudra the Brahmans have gratefully received lessons of Truth."

At this the yogi turned and walked toward the stall where the hunter stood with his back toward him weighing some flesh that lay in the scales. The yogi looked at the hunter and stopped still. This hunter was an outcast and unclean, a killer of cattle and bird, a handler and seller of flesh and he, a Brahman, could not go into his presence, much less go to him for advice. Yet she, the marvellous woman, had bade him go to him and see that which he would never forget and hear the words that would make him wise.

As he stood there, some hundred feet from the hunter's stall, pondering in uncertainty, the hunter put down his scales, turned and faced him, came directly toward him and bowed to him low. "O holy Sir," he began, "I have been awaiting thee. Yonder good woman sent thee hither to seek advice from me and thou, in thy perplexity, canst not make up thy mind to seek wisdom from one who is unclean and an outcast."

"How knowest thou all this?" faltered the yogi. "But a few minutes since I left the woman yonder. Here thou dost meet me telling me all that has passed between us and read the shrinkings of my heart and the promptings of my mind!"

"O Sir," answered the hunter, "Illumination and yogi-powers are mine too."

"What!" exclaimed the Brahman, "you, an outcast and a hunter, have spiritual powers? How came you by so great a blessing in these your low material surroundings?"

"If thou wilt come with me, holy Sir," humbly proposed the hunter, "and bless my house by the dust of thy feet, I will show thee how these powers came to me."

Wonderingly the yogi followed the hunter into his home, a mud hut, where, with reverent air, the hunter led him to a room in which an old man of peaceful mien and, at his side, a sweet-faced woman, sat on seats elevated as a throne.

"See," said the hunter, "these are my revered and beloved parents. These I have worshipped and loved and served all my life. These have been my earthly deities and to these I have given the strength of my concentrated love and homage from childhood up. And thus they, through my sacred devotion to them, have been the medium of my spiritual enlightenment. Yoga means joining the mind to the Holy Spirit, and when the mind is concentrated in a loving and reverent spirit upon something it worships as holy, it absorbs and is filled with the powers of the Holy Spirit, the energy of the Soul, called yoga-powers. Go thou back, holy Sir, to thy parents. Fill with love the void thou hast made in their hearts by leaving them in their old age. Satisfy them, give them thy loving and devoted attention, and the gates of true understanding shall be opened unto thee, and the wisdom and spiritual gifts thou seekest shall be thine.

"Look thou, Sir, my following the trade of a hunter is but a part of my devotion to my parents. While they live I shall do what they have done before me. And when my material services are no longer needful to them, when they leave me for another world, then I shall break my caste and enter into the glades of the forest to seek undisturbed my God in silence. But now my duty is here, and a blessed privilege is mine to serve in reverence these my parents, and walk in the laws of my caste uncomplaining. The realization of this and my adherence to it has alone been the means of my spiritual powers."

In reverent silence the proud Brahman heard and understood, and the jungle saw him not again at his accustomed seat until many years had passed. When he again came to that jungle, a kindly light gleamed in his face, and his glance was soft and full of love, for by the absolute and holy devotion he had bestowed upon the declining years of his departed parents, he had learned that love and duty to those nearest was the strongest lever to spiritual power and illumination.

THE EMPEROR AND THE SAGE.

Night reigned in the palace and all save the sentinels and night servants were tucked away in slumber. All save the emperor, he the king of all he surveyed, he the ruler of the many souls that dwelt in his land, he the owner of countless wealth, the lord and master of queen, prince, and subjects.

He walked the broad length of his luxurious halls and corridors, because he could not close his eyes in slumber and rest his weary brain from the problems of politics that filled it. He alone of all his palace was denied the balm that came to the lowliest and meanest of his people. Again and again he had thrown himself upon the rich softness of his canopied bed; he had counted the birds embroidered in his coverlet, had gazed at the jewels that studded the draperies which curtained his sleeping place. Yet sleep came not to his eyes, nor rest to his mind, nor peace to his heart.

Thus with wearied impatience he saw the breaking dawn spreading her broad hands in the east, and as he watched her push aside the heavy clouds of night, he spied just below his casement, the figure of a man lying on a heap of ashes in heavy sleep. "What!" thought he, "this poor wretch sleepeth in perfect soundness with naught 'neath his body but the refuse of the earth and naught for a coverlet but the canopy of night. Would I could rest thus even on my bed of down and with my cloth of gold to cover me."

For a while he watched the sleeping man and the breaking day, then in impatience threw open the casement and shouted to the sleeper: ."Tell me, O thou, how canst thou sleep thus without bed or house?" But the sleeper, wrapped in peaceful slumber, heeded not nor heard.

Then the emperor summoned his servant and ordered him to arouse the sleeper and bring him to his imperial presence.

The servant departed, but nearing the sleeper he saw in him one of the wandering hermits, who were known as ascetics or holy men, who gave great wisdom and carry with their wisdom blessings wherever they go. So the servant dreaded to arouse the holy man from his slumber, but having the command of the king to fulfill, he stooped over him, saying thus: " Oh holy sir, my master the emperor calls to thee from the casement of his palace. Much hath he been disturbed of late and little rest hath he found either by day or in the night, because of the weighty state matters. I pray thee, forgive me my rude awakening of thee and do thou answer make to his majesty the emperor, who calleth to thee from yonder window."

The ascetic arose, went to the emperor, and with a frown said: "Why didst thou have me disturbed thus from my slumber, thou imperial dog?''

The emperor smiled at this show of temper which, however, he knew was feigned, though rarely seen in the holy men of India, and said: ''Because, O holy one, there is that which I would ask thee and which I know thou in thy wisdom and kindness will answer. I have seen thy bed and envied it not, but when I looked upon thy sleep, deep and peaceful, I envied thee much, and I want to ask thee, how didst thou feel, when sleeping on thy hard bed of ashes?''

The hermit looked into the tired, selfish face of the emperor, then at the luxurious sleeping apartment with its settings of gold and jewels, with its bed of down and cloth of gold, and replied: ''In some respects equal to thee, in others better than thou.''

''In which way?'' asked the emperor.

''Why,'' replied the hermit, ''as soon as I fell into sleep I forgot my body and knew not what it rested upon. I forgot my bed of ashes and this oblivion made my bed as good as thy bed of down. But I felt better than thou after that, because my mind, being innocent of all cares, enjoyed all restful slumber, which was denied thee, thou imperial dog, thinking upon things which does not concern thy real self, but makes thy body to groan wearily, because of thy earth-filled mind.''

"Oh, holy man," said the emperor, "tell me, how can I, who am tired and wearied because of these warring elements in my heart gain this same sweet peace and sound sleep that is thine, thou who standest before me, clothed in rags and having no home thou canst call thy own, yet whose face bespeaks the calmness of untroubled waters, and whose body gives forth the glow of perfect health. Tell me, thou bearer of wisdom, that I may learn from thee."

The ascetic made answer: "By cultivating peace of mind, by giving up fighting another dog over a poor, fleshless bone."

THE HERMIT AND THE HOUSEHOLDER

In long past days when there were no books to teach men learning, but when men lived close to Nature and heard the Word of God from all the creation of God, when their ears were opened to His love and greatness; when their eyes looked into His face and saw therein the things that were made for them to see; in those days when men looked into their own hearts and saw there the law that was to guide their lives and lead their footsteps in the paths that He had made for them; in those days when men sought by the light from within what their relation was to God and what God's relation was to them, when they sought to read the laws of Nature and thereby learn the laws that ruled them; in those days there dwelt a King, rich, arrogant and puffed up by the idea of his great wisdom which, in reality, was not great at all, but much exaggerated because of his position. Nevertheless, he prided himself on his supposed wisdom and would summon to his court all the savants, pundits and holy men who were accorded great in wisdom, and woe to the man whose opinion differed from this fool who called himself wise, for his freedom was no longer his and often he died an ignoble death because his wisdom failed to coincide with this haughty, arrogant King.

One day a holy man was brought to his court, and among the questions of the King, this was asked, "Who think you the greater, O hermit, the hermit (sanyási), who goes into the wilderness alone to seek his God, dedicating himself, life and soul, to it, or he that remains in his home with family and seeks there to realize his oneness with the Father of All?"

Quick the hermit made reply, "The householder, O King, is the greater."

With a sneering laugh the King replied, "Then why are you a hermit? Why are you not a householder? You are an impostor and shall be made to pay for it. Here, my guards, punish him as he deserves. Take from him his freedom as a forfeit for his inconsistency and behead him."

"One moment," said the prisoner, "Tell me, O King, who you think the greater, the householder or the hermit? Pray, tell me this as I wish to be enriched by your knowledge before I die."

The King replied, "Why, a Sanyási, of course. He who leaves the world and all his goods to find his God in silence and alone is greater, yea, greater by far than any householder who lives in the world surrounded by the comforts of the household."

"If the Sanyási is the greater of the two," said the hermit, with a smile that spoke more than his words, "then why are you, O inconsistent one, not in the wilderness now, clothed in the garments of a hermit and seeking there to make your peace with God? By your own reasoning, should not your head too pay the penalty of your inconsistency?''

The King was startled into silence for a moment by the abruptness of the man's query, and the hermit continued, ''O King, since by your count, I am wrong, and by my count you are wrong, shall we not seek to find the solution of this problem so that each may know for himself who is the greater—the hermit or the householder?''

The King, who felt himself fairly beaten for the first time in his life, after some hesitation, accepted the challenge, and the very next day, disguised as a hermit, set out with the saint to learn by observation and experience which of the two were in the right.

Many miles they travelled and toward sunset they reached the neighboring kingdom where everything and everybody seemed in holiday attire. ''Come,'' said the hermit to the disguised King, ''there seems to be merry-making here. Let us see what it is that has brought forth these garlands and glad faces.''

Sure enough, following the people toward the palace, they saw a maiden, fair as the morning, attired in wedding clothes of rich silks, bejewelled with rare and wondrous gems, her fingers and toes stained with heiná, her tresses behung with pearls, standing on a low platform with a garland in her hands. Before her, in measured tread, walked an array of princes of high birth and great prowess, each gazing on her beauty, but each fearful that he pleased not the eye of the only daughter of the King, who stood thus waiting to find her choice of husband among the worthy princes who had been invited by her father, and who now passed her by in that procession of wooing.

One by one they passed her and still the garland failed to fall about the neck of the chosen one who was to be her husband and rule with her the land of her fathers. Proud and peerless she stood, smiling on one and all who passed, but finding in none of these the lover she sought, the lover who would be her lord and master, who would rule her and her kingdom, and not like these wooers who already had become captives and fallen slaves to her beauty and her power.

Then from out the crowd issued a young hermit, a youth with the radiance of innocence and faith in God gleaming in his eyes and on his face. And following the procession, he stood and gazed wide-eyed and boldly right in the lady's face. He saw her not as a woman, nor as princess, but as one of the beautiful things created by God whom he worshipped all his life. And thus he looked upon her, and she, seeing him without fear of her power and bowing not low to her beauty, threw the garland round his head and she, the King's daughter, the future queen of a kingdom, thereby made him, by the law of the land, her husband until death would them part and after.

Quick the ministers of state hurried to the young husband and bowed before him. But the youthful hermit heeded them not and strode on as if to leave the throng.

"Thou must to the palace," spoke the minister.

"Nay, I must about my business," quoth the hermit.

"The princess, thy wife, awaits thee," the minister urged.

"Wife! Palace! I know not of them," exclaimed the hermit, "but yonder in the green is my palace, and I wish no wife. Since childhood I have lived there in the wilderness and there will I die. I asked not to be wedded, so farewell, O King's daughter! I fly from thee and thy palace to live and die a Sanyási."

And so he left her, she so newly wed and forever widowed.

"See," said the onlooking disguised King in triumph to the old hermit, his prisoner and companion, "see the greatness of this Sanyási, who is not tempted by so fair a wife nor yet by the great honor put upon him. The greed of wealth and rank disturbs him not and he knows not the desire of pomp and glory. Rather would he dwell in forest glades and seek the wisdom of God in Nature's cloistered aisles than dwell among men honored and great. Was I not right? The Sanyási is greater than a householder."

"Judge not yet, O King," smiled the old Sanyási in reply, "but let us on."

As they left the wailing wife, the city of merry-making suddenly grew full of woe by the calamity that had come upon their loved princess. But the royal and holy searchers of the solution of the problem went toward the forest where night soon overtook them.

An hour later, cold and hungry, the King, sitting under a tree, said to the hermit who leaned against its trunk, as if in sleep, "I was a fool, O hermit, to follow thee in quest of wisdom. Surely, I would have shown wisdom to have remained in my palace where my bed awaits me and my food is ready. This is not to my liking."

But receiving no reply from the hermit, he gathered such dry leaves as he could find and made for himself a bed, and then searched about in vain to find a light to build a fire complaining all the while of the cold and hunger that overtook him.

Above them in the tree, two little parrots, as big as the clenched fist of a dainty maiden, sat and looked upon the intruders, and this is what they said in the language that birds use when they solve the philosophy of life:

"O little wife," said the one to the other, "thou, the best part of my home, awake, for wayfaring guests are below and one complained loudly of the cold. Oh sad am I that I cannot offer the warmth of hospitality! Grievous is the sin of my inability to make them comfortable. It is no doubt the fulfillment of my bad Karma that leaves me helpless in the face of my guest's discomfort!"

"Wait," chirped the little wife, "see, yonder is a light, perhaps a bonfire made by some wayfarer. I will go and bring a light."

And away she flew, returning with a tiny lighted twig. Deftly she dropped it upon the heap of dry leaves that the King had made.

"Hullo! Here is a fire!" exclaimed the King in delight and in a short time a blazing fire was warming his cold-nipped hands.

But soon again the King complained to the apparently sleeping hermit, "I cannot sleep while thou seemest to sleep so well. My hunger is too great for sleep. Would I were home so I might eat what is awaiting me."

"Hearest thou," said the husband-bird, "he, my guest, is hungry and there is nothing to feed him. What shall I do? Great is the punishment that awaits those who feed not the hungry at their door and sad is the plight that has overtaken my house when a guest is ahungered and is not fed."

Long they reasoned and bemoaned their lot when all at once the little husband-bird said unto the wife,

"It is the only way. Thou hast been a good and true wife to me. Thy presence has ever brought joy to my heart and luck to my house. Thou hast been all a wife should be. Farewell, and may thou be my wife in my next birth!"

And lo, the little bird plunged himself downward into the bonfire so that his guest that was hungry might be fed!

"Oh!" cried the King, "this is luck. Some bird dazzled by the flame has fallen into it. It will make a sweet morsel for my hungry self."

And depleting the little mainá of its feathers, he roasted it over the fire and ate it.

"But," said he, when he had gulped it down in a moment, "'tis but enough to whet the appetite, not to satisfy it. Would my hunger might be appeased."

And the lonely little wife-bird sat overhead and saw her husband disappear and heard the King grumble still in his hunger.

"O husband," she cried with plaintive chirping, "his hunger is not satisfied even by thy sweet self. I shall make thy sacrifice complete and fulfill the law of hospitality of this household."

And so saying, she drew her wings about her quivering little body and fell into the fire at the feet of the King.

"The gods smile upon me," cried the King again as he picked the feathers from the faithful breast of the little housewife. And roasting her over the fire, he ate the bird and fell into a sleep beside the still burning fire, an uninvited guest in the house of those who had given their lives for him.

With the waking dawn the King opened his eyes to find the hermit still leaning against the trunk of the tree, but his eyes were fixed upon him.

"Come," he said, "the day breaks. I will put you on your way toward your home."

"Why," said the King, "with the problem still unsolved, that we set out to settle?"

"It is solved," replied the holy man.

"Wherein," asked the King, "lies the solution of it?"

The holy one, who had dwelt in the jungle and had learned the laws of love and life on Nature's breast, told him of the little drama that had been enacted above their heads that night and the result of it. He, the holy one, at one with Nature and at one with God, had also been at one with the understanding of the little feathered householders.

"And I thought," said the King, with wonder-widened eyes, "pure chance had lighted the leaves at my feet for my warming and that better chance had thrust those two wee birds into the fire to stop my hunger."

"There is no chance, all is law," answered the wise one. "There was merit, O King," he continued, "in the young Sanyási thrusting the great honor of being a ruler of a kingdom and a King's wealth aside to go into the wilderness as a humble worshipper of God; yet he had from childhood thus lived, seeking wisdom and through wisdom he found happiness in renunciation and realization. But greater than he are those two householders whom these wee creatures represented to thee last night. Blessed, many times blessed, and of greater merit is the householder who, in the midst of turmoil and temptation, finds his at-one-ment with his Father and through that at-one-ment does his duty of a householder even to the giving up of his life to serve that duty. So, O King, thou seest that the householder and the saint are alike in spirit. One gives up worldly gain and retires into the wilderness to love his God undisturbed; the other, in the midst of worldly temptations, gives up the world to fulfill the duties of the householder."

ALL FOR THE GOOROO'S BOOKS

There was once a holy man who dwelt with his disciple in a little hut at the edge of a small village. Each day, at sundown, the villagers gathered about this little hut to hear the words of wisdom which this holy man spoke and to gain therefrom the strength to sustain their souls and live their lives in peace and love.

One day deep commotion reigned in the hearts of these simple people for the holy man had proclaimed to them that he would, on the following morning, start on a long pilgrimage to the holy places of the land. It would be four years before he would return to them. He blessed them all and begged them to be kind to his young disciple whom he would leave in their care, and told them to come each day at sunset as usual and listen to the words of wisdom that his disciple would read to them from the Scriptures. With loving hearts the villagers promised to do his bidding.

Next morning the Gooroo entrusted his beloved Holy Books to his beloved disciple admonishing him to take great care of them, and, above all, to guard them against the mice who oftimes played the mischief among them. Heavy-hearted and sad the young disciple heard all his injunctions, vowing within himself to guard his master's beloved books even with his life if need be.

So the holy one started forth on his holy journey and the disciple arranged the books in order and sat up all night in readiness to ward off the malicious danger of the mice, beating about the books with a stick to scare them away. And thus he passed the first night sleepless but alert for the coming of the enemy.

The next evening the villagers assembled to hear the disciple read the words of wisdom from the master's books, but the young man seemed tired and lifeless. Questioning him as to the cause of it, they learned that he had not slept because of his promise to his Gooroo to guard his precious Scriptures.

"Well," said the villagers among themselves, "bring the boy a cat to drive away the mice, so he can rest knowing the books are safe."

The cat was therefore brought, but with the coming of the cat, the disciple again became troubled because of the lack of milk to feed the cat. The villagers again put their heads together to remove this trouble of the disciple who had been entrusted to their keeping. They decided to give him a cow to supply the milk for the cat who was to guard the precious books of the master who had gone on a pilgrimage to visit all the holy places of the land.

Now the holy one had taught his disciple the worth of a cow, that the cow was the most sacred animal, the second mother of humanity, the nourisher of every human life in infancy, for is not every babe sustained by cow's milk, and above all, was not the cow the most loved animal of their Lord God? Krishna, Himself, when he walked on earth as a youth, had, on His own choice, become even a cowherd.

All this the young disciple remembered and remembering it, he worshipped the cow as a mother and served her with great care and fondness, and because of it he was not always ready to read to the villagers the wisdom they came to hear from the Gooroo's books.

"Now," said the villagers, "this boy, in his conscientiousness, is overly busy with serving the cow. Let us send to him the little Brahman maiden, who hath neither mother nor father to take from him the work of serving the cow, so he may be ready to read to us from the Book of Wisdom when we come every evening at sundown as the master bade us to do."

So it was that Brinda, the little Brahman orphan, first came to serve the Brahman disciple, and lo, at her coming, the house was filled with sunshine and tasks vanished from beneath her little brown fingers as if by magic! The hut echoed with her soft songs and the cow pricked up her ears and bellowed at her coming. So as time went on, the poor Brahman lad sat by the hour and gazed into the moon knowing not what the sweet pain was that filled his heart even more than the greatest truths that his Gooroo had given him, and oft, in the midst of his readings from the sacred Scriptures at sundown, he halted and sought in the crowd of peering dark eyes, the dancing ones with the downcast lids of the little Brahman maiden who came each morn to serve him and left him each eve taking with her the sunshine of his heart and hut.

And so time passed and soon the villagers noted that the disciple was in love with the little maid, and, because of it, he pined in the hopelessness of his position, for was he not an ascetic disciple of the holy man, and was it not expected, therefore, that he must never wed?

And so the villagers again put together their many and wise heads and took counsel among themselves.

"It is best" they decided in whispers. "The little Brinda is alone in the world. He is of her own caste. The holy man has made us guardians over him and since he pines for the maid and the maid for him, we shall have them wedded and that will be the best from all sides."

And thus the little Brinda became the wife of the disciple who lived in the hut and served the cow that fed the cat that killed the mice that threatened the books that belonged to the holy man who was on his pilgrimage to all the holy places of the land.

And the years passed and with the fourth there came again to the village the holy man who had traveled into many places to view the sacred spots on his pilgrimage. And he hurried to the edge of the village to find his hut and clasp again to his breast his disciple, the dear boy whom he had left in charge of his home and the books. But he could not find his hut. In its place stood a newly built house and around it all a wall that proclaimed it the home of a householder.

Wonderingly he called aloud to the custodian of the house and the disciple appeared wearing no more in his face the look of the ascetic but bearing in his left arm a year old baby and his right hand clasping the little hand of a three-year-old boy, who had the dancing eyes of Brinda and the look of the young disciple in their sweet faces.

On seeing the holy man before him, all the accumulated fears of his broken vows of the past years rushed upon his mind. He saw himself again in the little hut with his Master listening to the slokas that were to make of him also a holy man. He saw himself performing the holy austerities that were to lead to renunciation, he saw himself living a life at one with God in the wilderness. Then startled by this sudden rousing of old memories, he threw himself at the feet of his Master, rolled in the dust made wet by his rushing tears and cried:

"It all came about to save your books, O Gooroo! To keep away the mice a cat was brought. To feed the cat a cow was brought. To serve the cow the maid Brinda came. To save myself I married her, and these babies are the fruits thereof. All for the sake of your books, O Gooroo, all for the sake of your books!"

THE YOGI AND THE HUNTER.

A soft, brown fluttering thing—a bird with a shaft caught fast in its blood-spread breast fell at the feet of the ensilenced Yogi, who for hours had sat in deep meditation at the foot of a broad-branching tree in the green heart of a jungle. The hunter, following the path of his flying arrow, found himself thus confronted by the Yogi, who, rudely awakened from his trance-like attitude, looked upon him rebukingly.

Now in this land of castes and spirituality, he that is a slayer of living things, be they large or small, bird or beast, is out of the pale of all castes and is considered so unclean that his very touch is regarded as pollution. So great was the fear and consternation that overcame the hunter when he found himself before the Yogi, that he quickly prostrated himself to him and said:

"O thou holy one, forgive me for having intruded upon thy meditation. I know how unseemly it is for such as I, who make my living by the hunting and slaying of flesh, to come before thee. But I saw thee not, as thou didst sit in stillness. I saw only the bird perched upon the bough above thy head, and so intent was I upon its slaying that everything else was blotted from my sight. So I beg thee to forgive me and allow me to depart in peace. Do not follow me with thy anger, O Yogi, for having brought my unclean presence before thee."

The Yogi, looking upon him wrathfully, said:

"Thou hast aroused me from my silence. Thou hast caused a dead thing to fall upon me, thou hast polluted my atmosphere by thy unclean presence. And because of this, I could, by the power of my wrath, cause thee to die."

The frightened hunter writhed.

"But do it not, kind sir," he implored again, helplessly, "I pray thee, do it not. I know it for certain that though I fly to mountain heights or sink to the deeps of the ocean, thou, in thy wrath, couldst reach me there. So do it not, O spirit-potent one! I am too small for thy power. But ask any service thou wilt of me, for the expiation of my unconscious wrong to thee, and I will render it to my uttermost might. Only do not visit thy wrath upon me, holy sir, for the sake of my wife and my little ones, who would perish for want of life's sustenance if I am no more, for I am their only provider. If thou wilt forgive me and let me go, I shall never cross thy path again or come within a long radius of your holy seat."

The Yogi looked at the hunter with unchanged sternness and then said:

"Go thou, then, since thou wouldst serve me and thus escape my anger. Go thou far and broad into this forest and find thou my boy, my truant boy who comes not at my call, but wanders ever away, sometimes near, sometimes far, aye, ever in waywardness strays from me though I long for him. Go, seek him, find him and bring him to me. Krishna is his name. Call upon his name and he will come to thee and thou wilt bring him to me. Thus canst thou only escape the punishment thou so richly deservest, and return to thy home and people untouched by my wrath."

The hunter repeated the name slowly, "Krishna, Krishna." "Tell me, O Yogi," he asked, "how he looks, and I will hunt the jungle day and night and bring him to thee if he is to be found therein."

A slow smile of peace came upon the face of the Yogi, as he answered:

"The boy thou art to bring before me is of great beauty and grace. His garment is of rich and rare texture and gold in color. His complexion is dark, but with unchanging light of unwavering love gleaming from within until color is quite lost in the glory of that light. His brow is crowned by three peacock plumes, and in his hands he bears a flute upon which he makes strains of music that cause all hearts to throb in ecstasy because of its sweetness. This is the boy I will have thee find. And if thou art so fortunate as to catch him and bring him hither, thou shalt not only gain my forgiveness, but my blessing shall be with thee from now unto all life."

Happy in this given promise, the hunter rushed into the jungle calling the name "Krishna, Krishna," until the echo fell fainter and fainter on the ears of the silent Yogi who listened with a still smile on his lips.

And so the days passed until three were gone, when suddenly the hunter appeared before the Yogi, footsore and weary, and said unto him:

"O holy sir, I see the boy often when I call his name, but only as a flash, and then he is gone again. Oftimes, in the far distance, I hear the sweet strain of his flute as if in answer to my call. But ever, as I follow it, and seem to come upon him, lo, he is not there! And again from the far distance the flute I hear, and the flash of his garment I behold, and then, woe is me!—he vanishes, or is too far in the distance for me to overtake him. Once, O sir, I caught the flash of his eye. Oh, wondrous eye it was! And it seemed to me I must follow forever to again see the flash thereof. And I wonder not, O sir, that thou art sad, and wouldst have this wayward, but bewilderingly beautiful boy with thee. But I have come back to thee tired and worn, to tell thee that he eludes me ever, and empty-handed, my quest in vain, I beg thee to allow me to return to my wife and children, who ere now must have missed me sorely."

While the hunter was speaking, the Yogi sat gazing at him with wonder slowly growing in his eyes of wisdom, and when he paused, he said:

"Away, thou fortunate one! Bring to me this boy. Call upon him, follow him, catch him and fetch him to me, else never expect mercy from me."

And again the hunter hurried away, calling "Krishna, Krishna," until the jungle rang and echoed and re-echoed with that name. To and fro he rushed ever calling, calling, now chasing here now there, gazing into the thickets, peering behind the trees and anon crawling through the interlaced branches of undergrowths, until again the days and nights were passed. But he knew not of the passing because of the wild joy in the chase of the boy who lured him from the distances by the glance of his eye exquisite and the strains of his flute entrancing, until he once more stood before the Yogi. But this time he was not footsore or weary or frightened, but with flushed cheek, triumphant brow and glad voice he called forth:

"Here, O Yogi, is he whom thou seekest. Long and hard have I chased him, and ever and again hath he eluded me. But elusive and mischievous as he is, I have caught him at last and bring him to thee. For three days I followed the gleam of his golden garment, the flutter of his mantle in the breeze, the waving of his peacock plumes and the strains of his flute. Hither and thither he darted, flashed the beauty of his eye upon me, and then the splendor of his smile which quite outrivalled the jewel on his breast. But I have him now. I bring him to thee though he even now struggles to flee from me. But he cannot. I hold him tight. And now that I come to give him to thee, I cannot, I cannot; for his glance has made me forget the world, his smile has made me forget all that it holds, his flute has filled me with longings for that which only his beauty can satisfy. Though he is thine, O Yogi, oh let him be mine also. Let me stay here, I pray thee, to serve thee, so that I may be near him and look upon him always."

The Yogi stared at the glorified mein of the hunter who seemed to be grasping something which struggled to escape, but which the Yogi could not see. "What art thou saying?" he said, "I see no boy with thee. I see only thee."

"Why!" the hunter exclaimed in surprise, "dost thou not see thy boy, Krishna, whom I hold here? Come, take him, lest he escape again."

Intently the Yogi gazed toward him, and close at the side of the hunter, there flashed before his vision the outline of a figure—shadowy, faint, entrancing. It gleamed for an instant, then vanished, though the hunter still struggled to hold the figure beside him.

Then the Yogi rose and fell at the feet of the hunter and said:

"O fortunate one! O man that is blest beyond human ken! Thou art a Yogi of the highest rank and I am an outcast compared to thee. Didst thou call me a holy Yogi and thyself an untouchable pariah? The reverse is the truth. Whoever like thee has searched and reached and grasped the Holy of holies is the holiest Brahman, the highest saint, the greatest Yogi; and whoever, like me, has failed to do so, is a pariah, a false saint, and of unclean soul and body, though born a Brahman and trained in Yoga. It was to serve thee that I frightened thee, with mock anger, into turning thy mind from the killing of life to the Source of All Life, for I saw thee possessed of absolute concentration born of thy past birth. This I recognized when I saw how thou couldst see a bird above my head and yet not see that head, yea, couldst see only that bird to the exclusion of all else. I was right, for by the power of that absolute concentration thou hast in six days found what I have sought in vain in silent meditation for a life time. Dost thou know whom thou beholdest, O thou unconscious one? It is the Seedless One, yet the Seed of all Creation. He is the Lord of Love, the Youth Eternal and yet the Ancient of All Ages. He the Soul of the Universe—the Supreme Being in Manifest form, the Lover and Beloved of All—Krishna Himself!"

REAL RENUNCIATION.

The feast was over. The king had dismissed his royal guests and sought his chamber. Through the halls of crystal and jasper he walked, looking neither to the right nor left, noting not the beauty which surrounded him on all sides, nor the train of men that awaited the slightest nod of his head or wave of his hand, as a command. Straight to his chambers he made his way and passed into the inner richness, wherein it seemed all the beauty and luxury of a whole world had been stored.

But at the side of his bed he paused amazed, indignant and angered beyond expression, for resting in its silken folds, her hair disheveled, her toil-stained hands outstretched in languorous ease, lay a dark-browed maid. She, a slave girl, one of the meanest and lowliest of his household, wrapt in deep sleep upon the couch that had never held on its lap of down anybody save his royal self.

Quick he called his servants. "Take her and give her fifty lashes upon her bare back," was his stern command.

The slave girl sprang from sleep and stood before the king, trembling and speechless. Unpardonable her sin had been, she knew. But, oh, the work had been hard, and, tired beyond words she had been. On entering the apartment of the king to perform some menial duty, she had spied the luxurious comfort of that bed of gold and jewels, with its downy softness and richness, and a wild desire had come into her head to know just for once how it felt to recline thereon. So she had thrown herself upon it, and in that heaven of joy and rest that had come to her, and the seconds that followed, the girl had dropped off into an entrancing slumber, out of which she was now so harshly and roughly awakened by the anger of the king's voice and the brutal hands of the servants as they sought to lead her to her punishment.

For a second she turned at the door of the apartment as the servants were leading her away, then burst forth into a wild, shrill, yet silvery laugh. Peal after peal rang through the palace, waking the sleeping echoes of corridor and hall. Still more amazed, the king looked after the girl. "What!" thought he. "This girl pleadeth not for mercy, but laughs as if a rare sport confronted her and not punishment. What means it?" And turning to her, he said: "Why laughest thou, slave? Thy merriment soon shall become a dance of pain. Speak—why laughest thou thus?"

"Oh, your majesty!" she replied, "I was just thinking, if five minutes' sleep upon your bed of down and ease brings to my back fifty stripes, what would be the punishment to him who lieth upon it twelve hours out of each twenty-four, for years!"

Thoughtful the king became in an instant and, sending away his servants, said to the maid, who now stood before him pale and affrighted because of the boldness of her words: "O little maiden, slave thou art and lowliest of all my servants, thou hast taught me a lesson, and a teacher of great wisdom hast thou been unto me. Depart in peace, thou hast made me a wiser man this day!"

So all day and all night the king sat in silence, meditating on the words of the little slave girl. For the mistake of resting five minutes upon his bed, he would have commanded fifty stripes of pain to be given on the back of this poor child. Yet he, quite covered with blunders and mistakes, with sins and crimes, rested thereon one-half of his life! Was he worthy to enjoy all that his palace offered? Had he deserved all the blessings that had been showered upon him? Had he thought of others and been to them all that his position intended him to be? Protector of the people! Or had he lived only for himself, being shrouded in self, and thereby turned life into a curse for others and himself?

Thus he thought, and in the morning of the next day he threw aside his robes of state, his garments of wondrous richness, his jewels and trappings; and, robing himself even as the lowliest of his people, went forth into the jungle to sit and meditate, even as did the holy men and hermits.

A day and night passed and he had eaten nothing. Yet, though he felt hungry, he cared not for food, for so weary with self and overburdened with his sin had he become, that he cared only to be shorn from them. But in the noon hour of the second day, a man appeared with rich food and placed it before the king and begged him to partake thereof. Just then the king spied the figure of a hermit coming slowly toward him; and, pointing to the viands that stood beside him, he said: "Brother, wilt not thou too take of the food which this good man hath brought unto me, the unworthiest of all among men?"

The hermit replied: "Strange it seemeth to me that thou, who hath sat in meditation but for twenty-four hours, wouldst be honored thus! What is thy merit that the good things of life come to thee even without the asking, while I, who have lived in the jungle these twelve years, receive but the coarsest of food, and for that I must beg? I see but the greatest injustice and partiality in this, which in the world of the hermits should be entirely omitted."

Then he who brought the food, looked at the angry hermit, who in the bitterness of his jealousy had turned to go without even touching the food, and said: "O sir, this man but twenty-four hours ago reigned as king in a king's palace, with a king's power over millions of beings; but by the inner promptings of holiness he has resigned all his worldly power to sit here and meditate upon the power of the Most High! A life of luxury and ease and pleasure has he foregone, to live henceforth on the crumbs that fall from the table of a poor man. To a man of greatness and holiness have I brought food, begging him to eat thereof, that I might be blessed for the giving. And thou, O sir, what art thou? Ever a poor man thou wert, a grass cutter. Never hadst thou known aught but abject poverty and discomfort. Mayhap thou didst give up this meager life because of its material wants, to dwell here and meditate, thus receiving more of the blessings of life in flesh and spirit. But he, this pampered king of enormous wealth and power, hath given up a kingdom to become even the lowliest among men, while thou, a famished grass cutter, hath given up but a scythe, to become honored as a saint."

THE HERMIT AND THE VILLAGER

In a village of India, the land of learning and mystical lore, of picturesque princes and gentle-eyed peasants, there once lived a man who had an only son. Now, this son represented to his father all that was good and beautiful and wise, and often the father prayed in grateful fervor to the Lord of all Creatures for the blessing of this his only son.

It chanced one day that this rare son became ill and great were the lamentations of the father and greater still the fears of the mother when they realized that this illness which had overtaken their son could not be met by the man of medicine and herb that had been called to bring relief to the sufferer.

Now, at the edge of the village, near the foot-hills of the mountains, there had lived for years a hermit. The inhabitants of the village had looked upon him as a man of great holiness. So the father of the dying youth hastened to this hermit, and, after prostrating himself before him, said:

"O holy one, my son, my only son, lies dying. Pray, give to him the blessing of thy thought and touch so that health may come to him again and he may fill our home with gladness which is now shadowed by the wings of death."

The hermit looked upon the kneeling figure at his feet and, lifting up his eyes to the sky with a radiant smile, he cried:

"O Ráma! O God! All Thou doest is the best."

Whereupon the father of the sick boy grew impatient and said within himself:

"What is this! I come for consolation to this hermit who is known among the villagers as a great saint and he but answers my cry with this poor comfort that the Lord has done well to strike my loved one with illness, perhaps death."

And thus in deep discontent he left the holy man who raised his hand in blessing to him murmuring all the while, "O God! O Ráma! Thou doest all things for the best."

So the days passed and again the villager stood before the hermit, bent with grief and sorrow and said, "O holy one! He, my only one, is gone! The light of my house has vanished. He is dead and we are unable to bear our bereavement. Oh give me comfort, my son is no more!"

And again the hermit raised his eyes to the heavens and sang in praise, "O my God, O Ráma! Thou doest all for the best!"

At this the bereaved father waxed wroth and strode away vowing vengeance on the hermit who, he supposed, mocked him in his sorrow, for his grief had blinded him to everything save the pain of his loss.

That night, when the world was asleep and all earth was awake and the sky bent low to cover the sleeping children of the world with her health-giving mantle, the father strode forth from his home to meet the hermit who made so light of his great grief. He would punish him as he deserved to be punished. He would kill him, so that he would never more be able to give a stone where bread was asked. This hard-hearted hermit, he vowed to himself, should never more wear the cloth of a holy man and thus cheat the people in believing him a saint when in reality he was but a wolf in sheep's clothing.

Thus blinded to everything but his grief and the fancied insult put upon it, he made straight to the cot where the holy man was wont to sit in meditation and prayer at this very hour. But the hermit was not there. Contrary to his custom of many years, he had set out for the little brook where he was wont to bathe his feet and head earlier than usual and had remained there to see the coming of the night and watch the waking of the stars.

And thus he chanted his prayers at the brooklet while the enraged villager waited his return. The hours wore away and the inpatient madman at last remembered that the brooklet was a favorite haunt of the hermit. He had it, he said to himself, he would wait close to the brook and as the hermit would pass the thicket near, he would spring upon him and fell him to earth so that his mocking should cease forever.

Meanwhile the holy man, blissfully unconscious of the fate that awaited him at the turn of the road, walked along chanting his prayer and praising the Lord for the beauties of the night, calling down blessing on man and beast, when suddenly he stumbled, and would have fallen but for a tree upon which he caught himself. "O Ráma!" he cried, "thou hast done the very best thing! O Ráma thou doest all things for the best! It is a warning of thine, bidding me seek another road homeward." And turning, he followed back the road he had taken and plunged into the forest to reach his home by another path.

The villager saw and followed him. Since fate had played into the hands of the hermit this time, he would follow him and overtake him and strike him down with the club he carried with him even now. He kept the hermit in view, and, just as he was gaining upon him, he saw by the light of the moon the hermit plunge forward and disappear from sight.

Quickly he rushed to the spot and there found the hermit lying at the foot of a small hill, his face gleaming ghastly in the moonlight and the blood trickling cruelly over his brow. "O God! O Ráma!" he heard coming faintly from the holy man's lips, "Thou hast done the very best thing! O Ráma! Thou doest all things for the best!"

Like a flash the villager comprehended the deep meaning of those words as they reached him. The revelation struck him like a thunderbolt. So this was the man he in his rage would have slain, the man who, half buried 'neath a rock, cut, bleeding, perhaps dying, could still lift his hands in blessing and say, "O Ráma! Thou doest this for the best!"

As he thought this he hurried where the holy man lay and dragged him from the pressure of the rock, and, fetching some water, bathed his bleeding brow. Then he said:

"O holy one! Dark and deadly was the thought that prompted me to follow and find thee this night. Cruelly was my heart rent by thy words when I came to thee with a breaking heart over the loss of my loved son, and great was the rage that shook my soul and called out in vengeance against thee. But now I know and understand all thou meanest, thou who seest good in all the evil that befalleth mankind. Thou who seest blessing in the taking away of my son, as in the pain that now is upon thee. Forgive me, O holy one, do thou forgive me! Thee, whom I followed to kill this night, let me, oh let me lead to thy home."

"O Ráma!" cried the holy man, "Thou doest all things for the best! Thou hast given me a needle-prick in the place of a sword-thrust! Thou hast, in Thy kindness, thus thrown a rock upon me to avoid this man who, in the blindness of his wrath, would have killed me, Thy humblest and most unworthy servant. Verily, O Ráma! Thou doest all things for the best!"

MATCHING THE PEARL

A True Story of Hindoo Royalty.

The courtiers and ministers, the princes and vassal chiefs waited in the audience chamber for the coming of the King. But lately, Maharajah Amar Singh had mounted the throne of his fathers, he the last and youngest of the long line of uncountable Rajpoot Kings of Kishenpore. With his coming of age he had brought to his House a bride, a daughter of the Royal House of Radhpore, a maid as sweet and bright and winsomely fair as ever had reigned mistress and queen in the home of her lord.

And while those in the throne-room waited in covered impatience, he, the young Rajah, loitered in the innermost chamber of his palace and heard with delight the commands of love that fell from the lips of his little queen who ruled the kingdom of his heart with the jewelled sceptre of youth and beauty.

And well might he loiter in this bower of love where the lights fed by perfumed oil cast their glow and shed their fragrance, where the riches of beauty and luxuries of a realm were stored.

The walls were of marbled panels veined with soft rose and carved in curious designs and hung with soft silk of faintest gold studded with gems of crystal and jasper. The marbled floor was strewn with rugs and mattings that rivalled in softness, color and texture the blossoms that nodded and swayed in the courtyard beyond. The divans that lined the queen's chamber held in their lap a great profusion of cushions of downy softness embroidered in gold and silver and rose. On a raised dias, shrouded and canopied in silk, stood an ivory bed of wondrous and rarest workmanship.

No sound entered these chambers save the sweet voice of the queen and the chatter and prattle of her maids, or the sound of the singing fountains close by, or the wild outburst of the songsters sweet that lived to love and loved to live, or perchance the young King's merry laugh as he greeted his lady.

"No, no," pouted the queen, with the smile of Nature's most innocent coquetry wreathing her face, "I will not speak to you or give you a parting kiss till you promise to give me what I ask."

They stood with a broad sofa of gold and velvet between them and thrice had the Rajah gone round the couch to catch his queen for a last kiss before going out to the audience chamber, and thrice had she, Luchmee Ranee, eluded his grasp by running round the sofa and refused the kiss until he would promise to give her what she asked.

"But what is it, my tyrant?" asked the Rajah, admiring the color which suffused her cheeks, "What is it that you would have me promise?"

Luchmee Ranee pursed up her lips in still more tempting show as she replied, "But will you not promise first to give it to me before I make the request?"

"That is a cruel proposal, though not so cruel as this refusal of a kiss," answered Amar Singh with a laugh, "But, my little one," he continued with some seriousness, "I am a Rajpoot and King. My word is my honor, my honor my life. If I give my word, my life and honor are staked on it and both I lose if I fail to keep that word. Now, tell me what it is you ask, my Piari (darling), and I promise you that if it be in my power, I will make good your request even though it costs me half of my Kingdom."

"My heart's thanks for this," said Luchmee Ranee, as she bounded toward him and resting her head upon his shoulders, she lifted aloft, holding it between her thumb and forefinger, a pearl—large, white, lustrous, rare.

"Now pair me this pearl," she said, "that I may have the finest nose-ring that is ever worn by woman. My brother gave it me when I left his house this time and asked me to give it to you to pair."

"Is this all you ask, little wife?" the King laughed, "I was afraid it was something very, very precious or difficult to obtain. Your pearl shall be paired. Within the hour my keeper of jewels shall match that moti for your nose-ring. And now the kiss."

He took her to his heart and kissed her flushed cheek and laughing mouth. Then he left her and soon with his suite entered the audience chamber.

CHAPTER II.

Six months after the love-scene in the first chapter, Maharaja Amar Singh sat in the private garden of his young Ranee in solitary splendor. The wondrous growth and beauty of the tropical flowers he saw not, nor heard he the notes of gladness that burst from the throats of the little feathered creatures that lived in the trees and shrubs which surrounded him.

The peacocks strutted past him and then spread their gorgeous tails of brilliant eyes and walked by again in silent majesty. These the young king saw not, neither the tame parrots and doves who circled round him and sat on his shoulders as they were wont to do in other days when with his little queen he came to feed them and play with them and her like the child at heart that he was.

Now he saw them not, but brooded in heavy silence on the heavy insult that the House of Radhpore, the house of his dearly loved queen, had thrown upon his House, the ancient House of Kishenpore.

Thus he sat long, then took out from the pocket in the folds of his richly embroidered robe a pearl of wondrous lustre and size and looked at it long and earnestly and with a sigh thrust it back in the folds of his garment.

Within the hour the pearl had been brought back to him from its journey all over the broad land of India, and the messenger had said: "Unmatched I bring it back, O Maharajah, though I sought far and wide to pair it. Many there are that seem of its softness of lustre and sameness of size. But when I hold them close to this, my Lord, I find their shine does not match its fire, nor in size do they equal this. So I have brought it back to your Majesty once more to tell you, O King, that there is not a pearl to pair it in all the land."

Six months ago when the treasurer of his jewel rooms had said, "You cannot pair it, O King!" he had laughed a merry unbelieving laugh. "What! The House of Kishenpore unable to find a pearl to pair a pearl from the House of Radhpore!"

He would see. His little queen should have a pearl to match the one given her from her brother's house even though he searched the world to find it. Never had the Kishenpore House been unable to pair the pearl of the Radhpore House, and these two great royal houses of India had intermarried for centuries and each Radhpore bride had brought from her father or brother to her husband, the Kishenpore Chief, a pearl to pair for a nose-ring.

As he mused thus, the little queen with a train of brown-browed maidens emerged from the gate of the courtyard. Seeing her lord in silence and gloom she ran to his side quick as the birds that fluttered to meet her, and threw her sweet slenderness full in his arms.

"O my lord!" said she, "I waited long for your coming this day. Why wait you here when I await you there? Again the cloud on your brow I find. Tell me, my husband, what saddens your heart? What has taken the joy from your eye, the laugh from your lips and perchance the love for me from your heart? Has my happiness been too sweet that now a grayness seems to envelope it in a shroud? Tell me, has your quest of the pearl proved fruitless again? Oh seek not any more to pair the pearl, I beseech you. Would I had never given it to you. I care not for the jewel, my lord, much has it made me weep already. Oh, do give up the matching of it and take me again in joy to your heart as of old."

The young monarch was extremely touched by his lovely consort's sighing caresses and plaintive pleading. He kissed her with all the tenderness which her touching accent aroused in him.

"Hush, my moon," replied he in a husky whisper as he strained her to his breast, "hush my fairest! I fear I have not loved you enough, you whose lustre is softer by far than all the pearls that the sea has yielded to man. The joy of my love you are, the luck of my house, the loveliest ray of light that ever beamed on the heart of man. Come close to my heart, my darling Luchmee! Stay here and heed not my sighs nor the trouble that clothes my day.''

''But no, my lord, I can no longer bear it,'' burst out the Ranee in tears, ''Accursed be the pearl which has made you so sad and brought you such trouble. Accursed be this servant of yours who gave it thee to pair. Give it me back, I will throw it away or burn it into ashes. I will—''

''Nay, nay, that is too bad. It breaks my heart when you accuse yourself thus, dearest. It is no fault of yours. You understand not, my precious, that it is not the failure to secure you a pearl for your nose-ring that makes me sad, but the humiliation which it involves in another way. Ever have the Houses of Kishenpore and Radhpore maintained their honor by these pairing of pearls. No sweet daughter of your father's house, my lotus-eyed, has ever entered the house of my father as bride but she brought a pearl for her husband to pair, and never yet in the history of our house has that pearl been lacking till now when you, the brightest jewel of the diadem of maidens that crowned your father's house, have come to tread and make glad the home of my fathers. Until I pair your pearl, my flower, the House of Kishenpore, where you reign mistress and queen and which stands challenged thus, shall be shrouded in dishonor. This, sweet one, is my sadness."

"Oh!" sighed Ranee Luchmee as she nestled close to his side and hid her face in the folds of the royal robe, "Would I had never seen the pearl or never given it to you to pair since it robs me of the glad smile and happy love that was wont to greet me at each turn. But list, my dear lord, this day, because of heaviness of heart, my maids and I went in the early morn, even before the sun had opened its eye on the beauteous world, to a hermit, the holy one who lives close to the border of the jungle. To him we went and prayed that the joy would come back to your countenance again and the merry twinkle of love to your eye, even though the pearl be never paired. The holy man did bless us all and looking at me with loving tenderness, said, with his holy hand laid on my head, 'Grieve not, my sweet daughter. Your King, O little queen, shall match your pearl. One who is dark and of lowly birth shall give him the pearl to pair.' So I have come to you in hopefulness to tell you this. I pray you, O light of my life, smile and be glad again, oh, do."

Raja Amar Singh held her still closer to his heart and kissed the rosy sweet lips and spreading fingers. "Thanks, little wife," he said in a soft, melting undertone which was almost a sigh, "But much I fear me that your hermit mistakes, for over all the land we have searched for a pearl to match your own. Yet, get you to your chambers, my loveliest, and there I will greet you again when I have wreathed my face with smiles for your sweet sake."

And the little queen ran back to her maidens, forgetting for once to call to the birds that fluttered about her or to talk to the proud peacocks that strutted in majesty and poised, with gorgeous tails spread for her to view and admire. Nor stopped she to caress the shy-eyed fawn that plucked at her gown and rubbed the small palm of her hand with long, moist, quivering nose in appeal for the dainty rose-leaves which each day at this hour the queen was wont to feed it with. But straight to her innermost chamber she flew and prayed that the pearl might soon be paired even as the good hermit had said—not prayed that the nose-ring might be hers to wear—oh, no. She cared not for that even, though it rivalled in beauty and size the rarest of all gems that adorned the flesh of fair women. But she only prayed for its pairing that ere the sun was set she might behold again, in the eyes of her lord, the glad sweet smile that had ever been there and the joyous love that had crowned her life.

CHAPTER III.

Thus prayed Ranee Luchmee, sure in the faith that the pearl would be matched, for early that morning, even before the darkness of night had made way for the gray of dawn, Kamla, the eldest and most loved of her maids, had come to the side of her couch and roused her from her sleep. It was a light sleep into which she had fallen after hours of weeping wakefulness because of the sadness of her lord who had changed from a light-hearted boyish lover into a man of sorrow since the challenge hung on his House.

"Come, O sweet queen, rise now from your bed and we shall go to the hermit who sits in his cot at the skirts of the forest. A holy man is he and reads the hearts of all who come near him and wise is he beyond belief, and power has he over the minds of others for good. If you go to him and tell him of the sadness of your lord, who knows but he may help you and him by his power and goodness."

"But, Kamla," cried the little queen, whose eyes now shone like stars with excitement, "How can it be done? It is impossible for me to leave the palace. Never have I stepped on the breast of Mother Earth save in the gardens of my father and my husband. You ask me to go to the skirts of the woods; gladly would I go to the holy one, but how can it be brought about, Kamla; what will my lord say when I tell him of it or if he knows of it?"

"Leave that to me, my Ranee dear. No husband, king or subject, can ever object to his wife visiting the holy saints who sanctify even Mother Earth by their feet's touch," said the maid. "What the heart desires overmuch, that it will find. So come, put on these garments of mine for a disguise so that we can walk to the holy one in humbleness, and I am sure he will bring light to your eye which has been quenched since the heaviness has weighed upon your lord's heart."

Ranee Luchmee rose and soon dressed in the modest robe of her dear maid. A while after the keepers of the harem gates saw the bevy of sedate dark-robed maidens, with veils drawn low in front, pass through the gardens and courtyards and outer gates as they daily did at this time of the morning to have their ablutions in the sacred river and say their prayers and make their devotionals at its bank. Little did they suspect that their Queen with beating heart and trembling limbs walked in their midst. Close clasped she the arms of Kamla, for like a bird that is for the first time out of its nest, the little queen gazed at the breaking morn.

Never out of the palace-life the Ranee had drawn breath; for the first time in her short life had she seen the fields of the people and felt the dust of the road beneath her small feet. In wonder she looked at the cows that grazed close by, that lifted their great eyes with slow gaze to low at their passing. The calves skipped and kicked their hind legs as they neared them and the whistling cowherds with long strides passed them to make ablutions in the sacred stream. A few men and women passed their way toward the place where the holy man sat to receive from him blessings ere the labor of the day pressed upon them.

Many things she saw that were new and strange to the pet of the palace. Many things that were full of vague wonder sunk deep in her heart, that in the days of her riper womanhood would burst forth into thoughtful actions for those who walked in lowly paths.

At last they reached the cot wherein the hermit sat cross-legged. With eyes closed and a smile on his face as radiant as the breaking dawn that now shone through the thick of the forest, he gave counsel and blessings to those of lowly walk and those of high degree who came to ask for it. Many there were who waited but to hear a word from his lips as they told of the sorrows and burdens that oppressed their heart and to each and one he gave the word that brought hope to their eyes and spring to their steps.

All this the queen saw as she stood with her maidens a little apart, and she marvelled, as she heard the complaints, that such sorrow should dwell in this beautiful world.

Now swift to the feet of the holy man a young wife and mother came, with face drawn and haggard and eyes hollow and hungry. Bowing low many times to the dust, she pleaded, amid sobs and tears, "O holy one, for hope I come to you. Close unto death my husband lies. What will become of me and my babe if he is taken from our midst? Close to the heart of love you are, oh give me your blessing and tell me how to bring him to life once more. Poor are we and have not the wherewithal to purchase the food that will nourish and keep life in his body."

Sick and faint the little queen grew and with dilated eyes grasped the arm of Kamla. "Oh!" she whispered, "take this to her, this gold and note where she lives, that we may fulfill her needs."

Close on the heels of the little wife who kissed the hand of her who gave her the gold, came an aged widow, feeble and bent, who prayed that her cow be not taken from her, though she had not the food to feed it or her own weak self. And now a husband came and knelt at the feet of the hermit and in broken voice begged that the life of his oldest son be spared to him. Then a sturdy rustic pleaded that he might be made fit to take to his bosom the new bride that soon would come to his home.

All this the little queen heard with beating heart and tearful eye and her young heart turned with yearning pity to those who suffered pain. Reared in the arms of luxury, joy and love she had never known that beyond the walls of her dwelling there was a world unlike her own. The word poverty and its meaning was unknown in her vocabulary and no shadow of trouble had she ever seen until the smile had left her lord.

Yet what she saw here was grim poverty, utter hopelessness and darkest despair even in hearts as young as hers, as well as in those that had passed the years when hope springs into life anew. In that moment a vow was registered within her that relief should come from her hand to all who needed it.

"O Ranee," said Kamla, "go, make your prayer to him for all are gone now." And Luchmee left her maids and with hands folded and eyes cast down in sweet devotion she knelt at the feet of the holy one and bowed, touching the ground thrice with her forehead, and faltered in musical accents:

"O holy one! The boon I came to crave of thee has fled from my heart and in it a sorrow has come that is not mine own. I came to beg of thee the favor that by thy good and holy power the pearl of my father's House be matched by my lord. But now my heart has been saddened by what I have seen and heard at thy feet and now I pray to thee but to chase from the brow of my lord the gloom that lies there. And O holy one!" she cried with tears in her eyes, "sad have I been these days that my lord is sad, but never knew I the pain such as

I see aches in heart of man. Oh!'' she sobbed, ''would I knew how to succor them and make them joyous.''

The holy man laid his hand on her head in blessing: ''Little daughter! Even before the now rising sun sinks into rest you shall be glad again, for your pearl shall be paired by one who is dark and of lowly birth. And list, little Ranee! Because of your coming to me this morning, because the tears have sprung to your eyes for suffering of others, the hearts of those who rule this broad land shall be turned into kindness and all the poor of the Kingdom shall partake of good for your dwelling therein. Blessed are you for your tender heart, and all people shall call you so for the hand of charity you shall extend to all who need your aid.''

Bewildered, Ranee Luchmee bowed to the holy man again in deep homage, rose to her feet and joined her maids who again silently moved down the road toward the palace. A great sweet gladness rose in her breast, for that which she knew not before and now she knew.

CHAPTER IV.

Scarce had Ranee Luchmee gone than a shadow fell athwart the path in the garden where the young Maharaja was seated. Looking up to see who the intruder might be, he beheld at the side of the marbled bench one of the men who were known in that land as Minas.

Dark was his face, and a great wad of matted locks lay thick on his brow. His huge body was uncovered save for a loin-cloth that swathed his thighs. His eyes were bold and his features, though regular, were strong and rough. His muscles stood forth like the knots of the gnarled sal trees that dotted the jungle which is generally the home of his race.

One of the early and hardy people was he who lived in the hills of that land. Plunderers, highwaymen and robbers the Minas are by practice, and woe to the man who passes through their regions with gold in his bag or pack on his back by night or comes close to their huts by light of day. Innocent of letters or education, they are rough and uncouth in word and manner, ungodly in spirit and full of riotous living.

And yet place a Mina in a position of trust and responsibility and his life will he give ere he breaks that trust. The word "honor" the Minas know not, yet to break a promise or leave unfulfilled a duty of trust among these men of primitive living is all unknown in their history.

The King looked at the Mina and saw in him one who, as a child, had told him the easiest way to corner a wild boar and who had pointed to him that place in the jungle where the wild things herded. Many a time, when thirsty and weary in following a chase, he had wanted a drink from the spring of the rock, this fellow had shown him just where this cool water was to be found. Oft as a youth he had heard wild stories of adventures from this self-same man who now stood looking down at him with a rough kindness in his bold black eyes.

He bowed not to the king, for formalities the Mina knows not. A child of Nature, he is simple, plain, straightforward as an innocent child in speech or manner. Greed he had not, when filling an office of trust, and asking favors he dreams not about, and therefore he has no need of the low salaam which his civilized superior and the courtier made to rank or power. He broke forth in brusque tone:

"Amar Singh! I have just heard at the market place that your House stands challenged because you find no pearl to pair with that which your Ranee has brought from the house of Radhpore. Is that true?"

"Trouble me not," said the King wearily, "and bring not the gossip of the market place here, but best be it that your idle tongues dwell not on the honor of the House of Kishenpore or Radhpore."

"Ha! ha! ha!" laughed the Mina, so loud that the Rajah was shocked and looked up at him to rebuke him for want of manners. But as their eyes met, he dared not speak roughly to the man who, clothed in scant rags and wild in looks and manner, had the majesty of a freer soul than even a king in the light of those eyes.

"Ha! ha! ha!" he laughed again, "do you think it is a mind of curiosity that bids me speak to you, child? Did they lie or are you trying to conceal your trouble from me? They said there that you sent through all the land and found no pearl to pair the queen's. What a fool are you, Umra, not to ask me first about it! I can pair it or any you can produce within the hour by a gem of your own house. Did you not know that I am a keyholder of your secret vaults?"

The Rajah started and lifted his head again and gazed into the face of the Mina. Like a bird on the wing, the recollection came to his mind of the many stories he had heard in childhood, youth and even in manhood of the underground vaults and rooms full of untold treasures of gems that belonged to the kingdom of Kishenpore. But none knew where they were or were to be found or even who held the keys thereof. As often as he had heard he had put the story aside as a fable and a myth.

And now before him stood this rough man, worse looking than the poorest beggar, this Mina who possessed but a miserable hut, ate the coarsest of food, and covered his loins with a rag, who boasted to him with earnest mien and convincing tone that within the hour he would pair the queen's matchless pearl from the jewels of his own Royal House.

For a moment he was too staggered to believe it. Then he exclaimed, "Are you mad or dreaming, fellow, or are you playing the fool with my sadness, sirrah? It is true our House stands challenged for I find no mate to the pearl of my queen."

"Ha! ha!" the Mina laughed again, "Mad or fool or dreaming, bring your pearl and come with me, and within the hour, as I said, your sadness shall vanish. I will outmatch your queen's pearl in fairness or largeness or lustre. I will outmatch any gem in the land."

"One, only one will do" eagerly answered the King as he sprang to his feet and looked once more into the honest eyes of the other. "My good man, pair my pearl and naught you ask shall be refused you, even if it be my life, for life is not worth living with this dishonor on my House."

"Keep your rewards to yourself, for I want nothing," said the Mina with almost a holy smile of pride lighting up his rugged face. "It is with a dry piece of coarse bread and self-imposed poverty that our honesty and fidelity are seasoned. The key of some of the underground vaults of your House has been held by my family, handed by sire to son from generation to generation even as the throne and name of your House has gone from father to son. Even the Kings know not, yea, know not, who hold the keys and where are the secret treasure chambers. We do not receive any pay from your general treasury. There is a secret treasury of your House from which our small salaries, 5 to 6 rupees a month, are disbursed by the head custodian of this secret wealth, who is our chief, elected to this position by our common consent. But those few rupees are enough to keep me and my wife and children in rags, bread and salt—our only need and luxury."

The King looked at the Mina with awed wonder at which the latter said: "What are you looking at me like that for, Umra? Come, get your horse and take the pearl and let us be off to pair it."

CHAPTER V.

Soon the young king, unguarded and unarmed, at the side of the wild-looking Mina, was plunging through the jungles on the outskirts of which they reached the hills. All this way the Mina was running on foot with the Maharaja's horse, but here Amar Singh slackened the pace of the fiery animal into a walk and said, addressing his companion:

"How long hold you the keys of our vaults, and are you the oldest son of your father? And the gems of the vaults, when were they seen by my ancestors last?"

The Mina pushed his locks from his brow as he replied, "Ever since I was a boy I have held the key for the only son of my father I am. But had my father's eldest brother been allowed to live, I to-day would be stopping travelers in some jungle-paths away from your kingdom and relieving them of their purses. Anyway, I would not have been there inside that hut of mine to be near with the key in time of peril. The jungle hero is the life of a man like me, not the tame living of a man of trust as I am now."

"What mean you," asked the king again with an interested look at the wild man, "by saying that had your father's eldest brother been allowed to live? How died he?"

"Ah, that is a thrilling and sad story, Umra, would you like to hear it? You do? Well, you see this key that I hold was held by my grandfather who got it from his father. He lived in the hut where I now live with his wife, my grandmother, and their three sons. One day the King, your grandfather, passing by the hut, espied at its door a tree heavy with sweet lemon fruit. Being athirst he asked my grandfather for a fruit thereof. Quick his eldest son, a boy of twelve years, sprang forward to pluck the fruit and handed it to the King. Refreshed by it your grandfather called to my grandfather, saying, 'Here, twenty-two fruits still are on this tree. They are luscious and good beyond mine own fruits in my private gardens.

Let none of them be plucked but for me.' Thus commanded he and rewarding my grandfather and his sons right royally the king and his train rode away. Each day the king's man came for one fruit and each day my grandfather plucked and handed one and watched the tree and counted the fruits that none might steal them. Alas, the cursed lemons, the cause of such a disaster!"

"What disaster?" enquired the King, as he saw the tall black man's eyes became almost moist as he stopped speaking, a little overpowered by some sad feeling.

"Well, I will tell you, since you wish to hear. One day my grandfather went to the market and on his return counted the king's fruits as was his wont. He had daily cautioned his wife and sons to be wary that none might partake of the fruits. Every time he counted them they were all there. But this time he found one fruit gone. He asked his wife, she knew not who had plucked it. His two younger sons looked in his face and shook their heads for they had not eaten any or seen the culprit. Then my grandfather's face grew stern and hard and he called his eldest son to him, he the first born and most beloved. 'Child!' he said, 'have you stolen the King's fruit?' The boy dropped his head and looked aslant at the father's enraged face, and then put out his hands in supplication for mercy. But the father saw it not. He only saw the stains of the fruit's juice on the hands and caught its sweet-sour fragrance from the breath of his boy. Instantly his eyes grew big and round and red with rage, and grabbing his sword from its scabbard, he cut the head of his first-born quick and clean from its trunk."

"What! Cut off the head of his boy for eating a lemon? What a madman he was, your grandfather!" exclaimed the young Maharajah in excitement.

"Ay, ay, so also said your grandfather," promptly answered the Mina. "Then taking his child's head by the locks my grandfather rushed six miles down hill to the King who sat in state in his audience-chamber with princes and ministers and courtiers about him. 'Horrible, cruel, brutal!' the king gasped, as he shuddered, 'the man is mad! Kill a child for stealing a fruit! Why, man, are you mad?' as my grandfather held the head of his first-born on high and shouted in frantic pain, 'Kill me, if you will. I have done it! I have done it! I have killed my first-born!' 'Madman!' cried the king again, 'why have you done it? Dear to your heart was this boy and comely to look upon.' 'I did it, I did it!' the frenzied man cried, 'I had to. He was my first-born and dearest of the three to my heart. But I hold the key of the underground vaults of your secret treasure and he my eldest should have held them next. But how could he? How could he, a thief now at twelve, and stole from his king? How could he live to receive the keys of the vaults from my hand? How could I trust him, a thief, with the keys of a trust that has never been broken by so many generations?''

The Mina paused and then added with a sigh, ''And that is why I hold the keys, I who am the only son of the second son of my grandfather. But here we are. Now, dismount. Let me tie your horse to that tree and your eyes with this band.''

CHAPTER VI.

''Bind my eyes? Dare you do that, you knave? What do you mean by it?'' shouted the young Maharajah, his pride wounded by the proposal of his ragged menial to put a band over his eyes.

The Mina laughed a hoarse yet jolly laugh.

''Then,'' he said, ''you need not go with me. You can go back with the pearl unpaired and your house disgraced. I will not take you there to the vaults without first blindfolding you, though you be the king himself. It matters not who you are.''

''But,'' demanded the King, ''what is the reason? Why would you blindfold me? Tell me that.''

''Because,'' replied the Mina in a gentle yet firm tone, ''because you must not know the direction or the location of the vaults. None has known it nor ever seen it since my time. I will show you the vault to select your pearl because your house is in disgrace, and I am in duty bound to save its honor. It is a case of those emergencies in which we have been told to yield something of our treasure trust. But are you going to get your eyes bound, or are you not?"

Amar Singh had no other alternative but to dismount. He also saw the wisdom of the reason the Mina gave in explanation. What jealous, faithful guardians these were of wealth committed to their charge on simple trust, he thought to himself. What a rare example of the veriest soul of honor and fidelity encased in almost a savage body clothed in a ragged loin-cloth. That honesty worthy of the highest saint could dwell in a poverty-stricken low caste Mina, the young King thought he could never imagine.

His heart was also heavy for the fate of the young culprit of many years ago, of whom the Mina was just telling him. "Poor little lad!" he thought, "because he stole and ate one of my grandfather's fruits he lost his young life, and that by the hand of his own parent. What rugged justice and yet what a noble spirit!"

But here the cloth was about his eyes and the Mina was leading him through what seemed a tunnel. Then down flights of stairs, up inclines, down more stairs where it was damp and the atmosphere was chill and moist. Now again he was treading upon creeping things and flying things flapped their wings over and around his head and something brushed by his legs.

But ever he felt the hand of the Mina about him or halting to strike fire from a flint and light an oil lamp which he knew by its smell. Now through another labarynth of crooked paths and winding tunnels.

Here they halted and the Mina took from his belt a key and the King heard him open a heavy, clanking door. Now through other chambers that were full of the smell of everlasting dampness and then a halt again, and here the band was snatched from the King's eyes and he stood in the chill of an underground vault.

The Mina opened the lock of an old rusty iron chest and pulled and threw back the lid.

"Now look," said he to the Rajah.

"Look? Look at what? I can't see anything. All is dark to me here," said the Rajah.

CHAPTER VII.

"Here you are at last, Umra!" cried the Mina in a merry voice as he watched the face of the King, "chest after chest and vault after vault of gold and precious gems of different kinds and qualities rare this underground world does hold, and all belong to the House of Kishenpore. Now take your pearl to pair."

At first all was indeed dark to the King. Then little by little he saw, by the faint rays of the poor oil lamp—ay, piles of lustrous, glowing, gleaming pearls!

With a cry of joy and amazement he looked upon the contents of that chest. Thousands upon thousands of pearls, large and small, lay heaped up, catching and repelling the rays of the smoking oil lamp, and filling the vault with their light.

Pearls of all sizes, kinds and lustre greeted his eyes. Pearls that were milky white and dazzled the eye by their sheen. Pearls of creamy softness that held in their hearts the color of rose. Pearls were there that flashed back the gold of a star that was lost, or held in themselves the bluish gleam that is struck from a flint. Pearls of gray that seemed darkened by tiny clouds of smoke and pearls of inky blackness all piled in heaps before him.

Forward Amar Singh sprang and took one, far larger than the size of the pearl he had come to pair. Then delighted he stooped for a handful of the white ones.

In an instant he was caught by the hand and a short sword the Mina held close to him.

"Only one, my master," cried the Mina, "that is all you asked for. Why did you lie, if you wanted more? You said you wanted one and you must take one. Had you asked for more, you might have taken them.''

The young King was now really vexed and disappointed.

''Are they not mine?'' he asked in astonished imperiousness.

''Yours to use,'' said the Mina, ''only when your House or your State is in peril or in need of funds for its safety or for the sake of its honor. Until then I hold the key, and not even you dare take from this treasure-store more than the need of the moment. Your House now needs this pearl to save its honor. Take your pearl, whichever one you wish, but only one it must be. For the rest I hold the key.''

The King took his pearl, one of wondrous perfection, whiteness and lustre, and gazed once again on the scene which rarely meets the human eye. He was now blindfolded again and led through all the winding tunnels, chambers, up-and-down steps and corridors back until the sweet air of the earth's surface touched his brow and hands again and the Mina removed the band from his eyes.

Taking the King to his charger, the Mina said cheerily: ''Now back to your Ranee with your pearl that will pair any jewel of the Houses of all India.''

Amar Singh embraced the Mina and assured him he would never be able to repay this debt of obligation to him for thus saving the honor of his House.

"Ha! ha!" laughed the Mina, "that is a good joke. How are you obliged to me? The treasures are yours, so is the pearl. I am only their keeper."

"But I never knew of their existence and you have given me the pearl which my money could not buy in all India. I take it as your noble gift, O my more than noble Mina!"

Saying this he again embraced his wild menial more cordially than ever he embraced a brother and leaped across the saddle. Then with his old glad joy in his eye, the young wild love in his heart and a sense of honor untouched throbbing in his soul, he forgot the youth who had died because he had stolen the fruit a king had chosen, forgot the gems in the underground vaults like rays of moon-beams, forgot the Mina whom he left now far behind, forgot all as he urged his horse and rode straight to his palace.

He only thought of the pair of pearls in the folds of his cloak, and the far fairer pearl, his little queen, who knelt in prayer that her dear lord might find the pearl to pair, so that the light of his love might wreath his face again and bring him in joy to her arms very soon.

* * * *

Again in the innermost chamber, in the perfumed bower of love, the King clasped to his heart his precious queen.

"Your brother has given a pearl to pair which paired I give to you again. But had he bidden me to pair this rarest pearl of womanhood, I would have searched the earth in vain for its match, and Kishenpore would surely have been disgraced forever."

THE OAK AND THE VINE

Once there grew a little tendril
  From the heart of Mother Earth,
And she strove with all her power
  To break from her prison berth.

So she lifted head and shoulder,
  Thrust them free into the world,
And she caught the smiling sunbeam
  As her tender leaves uncurled.

And the soft rain fell upon her,
  Washed her fresh and eager face,
And the breeze's sweet caressing
  Filled her with a nameless grace.

So she strove through all the springtime,
  Happy in her youthful strength,
And her leaves grew thick and darker,
  And her roots grew firm at length.

So she leaned far in sunlight
  From an oak tree standing near,
And she heeded not his warning
  When he whispered, "Grow thou here,

"Where my arms can spread above thee,
Shield thee from the sun's hot glow,
Save thee from the storm and torrent
That will lay thy beauty low."

"No," she laughed, "thou knotted oak tree,
Far too rough and coarse art thou
For my frail and tender beauty
To entwine thy gnarled bough.

"Thou art old and hard and wrinkled,
And thy sides are worn and gray.
Why shouldst thou dare to address me?
I alone must live my day."

So the Oak Tree turned in silence,
Drew away his rugged hand,
But he knew her fragile beauty
Was not made alone to stand.

He, the King of all that forest,
Knew each vine must have an oak,
And a deep and mighty pity
In his heart for her awoke.

Then he pined too for the clinging
Of her soft arms young and fair,
And her tender, close caressing
On his trunk all gray and bare.

But the vine was proud and wilful,
  And she laughed and turned away,
Flirted with the bees and blossoms,
  Played with them through all the day.

And she sang with birds and breezes
  As they kissed her spring-wide eye,
With the butterflies coquetted
  As the spring days frolicked by.

Then one day the early summer
  Burst upon the waiting earth,
And the tripping, lisping springtide
  Suddenly had lost its mirth.

And that early child of summer
  Grew apace with rapid stride,
Down she came from southern hillside
  With her sunflag floating wide.

And her heat beat on the flowers
  Till they fell low with a sigh,
And the birds sat in the quiet
  Of the Oak Tree standing by.

And the bees' persistent buzzing
  Dully fell upon her ear,
And the breezes too were absent,
  Butterflies came not to cheer.

And the high noon in the heavens
  Beat its gold upon her head
Till the Vine in blasted beauty
  Drooped upon the ground nigh dead.

Then she gazed upon the Oak Tree,
  Standing there so strong and tall,
And she longed with bitter longing
  At his sturdy feet to fall.

Just to feel his shadow o'er her,
  Just to hear his rustling voice,
Just to grasp his rugged branches,
  In his mighty strength rejoice.

Then, O lo! the breezes lifted,
  Gathered strength as on they fled,
Till the winds of all the heavens
  Shrieked about her quivering head.

All the forest bent and staggered
  'Neath the fury of that gale,
And the thunder crashed and bellowed,
  Lightning flashed o'er hill and dale.

And a cold blast from the hillside
  Struck the vitals of the Vine,
And she cried, "O, Oak Tree, help me,
  Death doth chill this heart of mine."

Then, O see, the little tendril
  Suddenly is borne on high
By her friend the sturdy Oak Tree
  Who had heard her plaintive cry.

He had braved the storm to reach her,
  In her attitude forlorn,
Though his roots had cracked in bending,
  He now soothed her body worn.

Oh, she clung with loving fervor
  To his rugged, battered arms,
And her heart was full to breaking
  As he stilled her vain alarms.

So upon the hillside yonder
  Grows the Oak Tree strong and fine,
And about his rugged grayness
  Twines the beauty of the Vine.

And the wild things of the forest
  Find within their shade a home,
And the Vine warns every tendril
  Who would leave her oak to roam.

"For," she says, "in all the forest
  Every Vine an Oak must twine,
And the Oak Tree strong and sturdy
  Needs the twining of the Vine."

THE MOON-MAIDEN

A Legend of Old Ceylon.

It was in the old days that are gone down into the sea where the singing-fish sing lullabies to them always in the seaweed groves, when the seas were first churned and Lakshmi with her twin gifts, Beauty and Sorrow, was born; before the Asuras, those proud old Titans, ever rose up in their wrath and dared to war with the Gods; before ever the last Buddha in his hare-days was made hare-prince of the Moon.

It was in the very old, old days, and the Moon was always full, and shone with quiet peaceful rays upon the men that knew no sin; when Chetiyah was king of Damba-diva and borne up always in mid air by the four gods, before he told the lie that drove them all away, so that he fell to the outraged Earth that shrank back from his pollution and opened a great fiery chasm, so that he went down quick into A'pa, the lowest hell.

And every night, when the winds held their breath to hear the whispers of the gods as they walked in the still Earth-Garden, the Moon-Maiden came down through softest fleece of lightest clouds, and bathed her white loveliness among the lotuses in the Restful Lake. But the Restful Lake was lost long ago, when the Moon-Maiden fell in love—mortal love, as I shall tell you now.

Only we know that it lay somewhere in Lanka's (Old Ceylon's) wooded depths, wrapped round in mirrored stillness, always.

Every night she used to lie floating, whiter than the lotuses that clustered round her, with diamond-flecked leaves, tenderly, while the waters kissed her eyes and brows and cheeks, telling her all their dreams of quiet thoughtfulness, perfect peace; and many a god came down to the shores of the Restful Lake to woo her for her bright beauty, night after night, singing his sweetest songs through the reedy sedge. But always she shrank back, cold and chaste, into the coyest veil of lotus-cups, and would not hear.

And so the ages ran on, and the Moon-Maiden was a maiden still, unloving, though all-loved.

But for many a night, unseen by her, there had been one watching with reverent gaze, young Prince Chulani, the brave hunter, whom all the maids of Lanka sighed for, all in vain. For he ever left song and feast, and wandered into the still wood alone, longing only for the fair vision in the waters of the Restful Lake.

And the weeks sped on, and the months sped on, and still he could only watch from the tangles of the mango groves, seeing always, but daring never to be seen. Till one time a great longing seized him, and he rose up swift and silent from his ambush, and stepped down into the dim waters, and with strong arms clove his way stealthily to where the Moon-Maiden lay, all asleep with the low whispering of the waters. And close to her cheek he laid his own, and twined her long hair round his brow, and breathed, fearful yet brave, into her ear, "Oh, Queen of all my dreams, awake!"

But over the frightened waters went a shiver, and the lotuses closed their cups for fear, and the sedges hushed their lullabies and the Moon-Maiden was gone, far away back to the black-blue sky through the shielding clouds of her mother Night.

But he went away mourning many a weary day, nor ever to the Restful Lake durst go again, but always with heavy brow he brooded apart in the halls of the palace, heedless of hest of king or smile of maid: and all the people looked sorrowing on their changed hero, who wrought no longer feats of arms, nor deed of chase, nor any noble thing.

Now the king's High Priest, Seneka, who knew the songs and tongues of every bird, and read the rede of cloud and star, saw all this sorrow that had come upon Chulani, and how he forsook the worship of the holy gods: and he called him to him alone in his secret chamber, and made him tell him all his grief.

And when the tale was told he was sore amazed, and for three days took counsel with himself, and with the Parrot-Pandit, wiser than all birds.

"Much hast thou dared, O Chulani, for mortal to love deathless maid: to her death never comes, for she is Amara-dévi,* but thou, like all mankind, must die. Yet I have found a way whereby thou mayst win the love of the bright Moon-Maiden, so only thou hast skill and daring for the deed that must first be done."

Then Chulani spake short and joyful, "I dare all, and she shall give me skill!"

"Then hearken to me. In the land of the Nága King, beneath Samanella Kanda,** the butterfly hill, whither twice a year the troops of butterflies wing their way to bow down before the great Nága, there lies a huge cave, deep and dim, wherein the Nágas keep their magic treasures. And all day long, and all night through, a seven-headed Nága keeps the door, watching always with sleepless eyes lest any steal away their hoard. And in the seventh head of this Nága is the Wishful Jewel; this, if you canst win, thou mayst gain all that thy heart longs for—all save immortality only; that one gift the Nágas cannot give. But

*"Amara-dévi" means "The deathless lady."

**"Samanella Kanda"—"Butterfly Mountain;" this is Adam's Peak. A common phenomenon in Ceylon is the pilgrimage of hosts of butterflies, mile after mile flying towards the Peak. The Buddhists say they go to pay homage to the Sri Pada or sacred footstep of Buddha, but long before Buddhism, in the days when the Nágas, or fabulous snakes, held the hill country of Ceylon, the butterflies went the same journeys, for the benefit of the Nága Rajah.

think well ere thou resolve. For like should ever mate with like, and what hath mortal to do with love for the Immortals?''

But Chulani was young, and heeded naught of thought or care, nor prudent saws. Only his breath came quick and his eye lightened as he heard of the Wishful Jewel and the Nága monster, and he laughed out for very joy of love and enterprise, ''Aha! Now will I slay that seven-headed Nága, and win that rare jewel of his, and the Moon-Maiden, the white-browed Amara-dévi, shall be mine even yet!—all mine!''

And day after day, for two whole weeks, he worked hard with the King's chief armourer, forging arrow heads of bluest steel, and sturdy shafts of toughest teak, and a great round shield with many a mystic word inscribed. And in the end he started forth on his long journey to the Nága land through the waste of unknown jungles and long sand-blown plains, while the people all came down thronging to the city gates to see him go, and many a maiden held her breath, peering through her lifted veil, watching the gay young hunter as he went, and thinking sorrowfully how they would never see him again, but the serpent's fiery breath would scorch his fair beauty into hideous death.

But he strode stoutly on. Day after day through slumbrous shade of heavy-hanging creeper-clustered trees, where the fierce sun's rays could scarcely pierce, and always dead silence of utter loneliness brooded over gnarled windings of twisted roots and giant trunks, so that scarce two fathoms of this way might be seen; only the butterfly pilgrims floated lightly overhead, and he knew well that their way was his, and their track would never err.

And at night the thick darkness came down, and the trees sprung into sudden life of myriad insects' hum, and far away he heard the boom of elephant, and wandering jackal's cry, while every branch and every creeper hung and swung in fitful shapes around him, till they almost seemed to teem with life, and whisper in low words that he might not know, of how the way was perilous and long, and the end of all uncertainty, or certain death; and were there not damsels at home as fair and rare as any dream-maiden in a haunted lake? But he shut his ears bravely, and would not hear, looking only up to the sky he scarce could see, where she, his queen, smiled brightly from the placid depths through silver canopy of cloud and milky way.

And all his heart went up, "My love, thou shalt be mine!" and fear and loneliness fled away.

So many a day he journeyed, till the thick jungle ended and he came to a great salt stretch of sand and salt, blown over always by the hot east wind that burned, and blazed, and scorched; here was no life nor track of living thing, nor any shade of scantiest tree, nor green of herb, nor gleam of water, but all one dreary desolateness; and the red daze of heat hung over on the copper sky.

And for two days, faint with thirst, he struggled on, hoarding the scant water in his gourd with jealous care. But on the third day it was all finished, and the sun beat down on his bowed head with pitiless power, and his eyes were dim for utter weariness and glazing glare, while his parched tongue clove close and dry to the roof of his mouth; and in the end he sank down on the hot sand, death-stricken.

But his time was not yet come; and in a while he was half roused, hearing a pleasant rippling of running waters, and sough of waving trees; and over all a sweet low song, sung in his own tongue, but in voice so sweet as never mortal sang.

And for a long time he lay, not daring to open his eyes lest it should be some false mirage; but still the song went on, and the burning heat and pain were gone; and he said to himself: "Now am I surely dead, and have changed into some other stage in the long soul-wandering;" and longing much to know into what he had transmigrated, he sat up and gazed around.

But he was a man still, his very self it seemed: but all around him instead of desert waste was greenest verdure, and long carpets of such flowers as never in his life had he seen before, and scented trees bent over him loaded with bright fruits and blossom both at once, and through the vista of their arching he beheld the fair glinting of a clear rippling streamlet, purling happily to itself of all the bright sights it had seen, and all the good deeds it had done to the thirsty earth.

And on the tree just overhill were two figures—Bird-Maidens they seemed, with fairest faces of Lakshmi's daughters, and long floating hair that wound round softest bosoms that swelled into tenderest song as he sat listening, and lithe throats with fullest sweetness curving; only all the rest of them was bird's plumage, soft and rare as bird of Paradise.

And when they saw how he was awake and wondering, the twain flew gently down and sat on either side of him, fluting still their silver melody, singing of rest after wandering and love, and gazing upon him with long eyes, lid-shadowed, till Chulani felt all life revive, and he stretched out his hands to them, and said "Tell me, sweet saviours of my life in the waste wilderness, who are ye?"

And they, singing still, murmured, "We are the Kanduro, the Bird-Maidens of the Passing Hour; and we sing always of how the skies and woods and life and love are bright and young, and we take no thought of morrow or sorrow, but fly always floating after the pleasures of the passing hour. But who art thou, O youth? and whither dost thou journey through the desert of Trackless Land? We found thee dying and fainted, but thou wast too goodly to die, so we bore thee upon our wings and brought thee to the fair haven of the Passing Hour."

And he answered, "I am Chulani, from the palace of king Wédeha, and I go to the land of the Nága king to slay the great seven-headed Nága, and win the Wishful Jewel."

Then they leaned over him, and smoothed his ebon hair lovingly, "But what hast thou to do with Nága or Wishful Jewel? Why shouldst thou die? For thou wilt surely be slain by the poison-breath of the Sleepless Monster. We have heard full many a tale of many a one slain by him."

But he laughed short, "Die or live, go I must; for I love Amara-dévi, the moon-maiden, and in no other way can I win her, save only by the Wishful Jewel."

"Amara-dévi? oh, we have seen her often; cold is she, and white, and proud, and heeds naught of swain or love. Rather stay with us and dwell ever in our pleasant land, and wed with us; no scornful damsels are we, but always we love the brightness of sweet youth and joy. And thou art all too fair for such as she."

But he was steadfast, and would not stay.

Then the Bird-Maidens sang again, a sleepy song of restfulness, bidding him at least rest while on his toilsome way ere he went on through the scorched desert of the Trackless Land. And because the way was long, and he sore wearied, he consented to bide one day in their pleasant bower beneath the green trees by the purling brook. And they kissed his tired eyes, and sang again to him, and fondled him to sleep, weaving a drowsy charm of magic melody.

And never would he have waked again from the slumber to which they had lulled him, but that the Parrot-Pandit, who, sent by Seneka, had always followed him unseen, now came, and perching in the foliage near screamed thrice with the scream of the eagle-king. And the Bird-Maidens flew off for fear, leaving him there on the moss-grown bank asleep, ere yet the charm was ended.

Then the Parrot-Pandit flew down to Chulani, and spake in human voice, "Awake, awake, Chulani, rouse up quickly! Thou art in haunted land, and the Kanduro will lull thee into endless sleep, far from fame and friends, and enterprise and home, and thou wilt slumber on, a laggard nothingness, for all eternity. Awake, wake! Arise and fly, while yet there is time."

But the charm had well nigh worked, and Chulani was hard to rouse; but at last he rose up sighing, and went on with lingering steps, and immediately stream and grove and pleasant shade had faded far away, and he was toiling painfully on once more through the burning sand. And the

Kanduro, changed now into foul vultures, came flying after him, flapping with noisome wings around his head, waiting till he should fall fainting to feast on his carcass.

But the Parrot-Pandit still kept near him, and gave him a seed, round and red like olinder; and straightway Chulani felt his strength revive as the strength of ten men, and he shook his arrows at the foul birds and spake wrathfully, "O false Bird-Maidens, now do I know your foul vileness! Fain would I slay ye, only that these shafts are for the Nága monster only!"

But they screamed wrathfully, and flew off to tell the Nága king how one was coming to slay his guard and steal the Wishful Jewel away from him.

And now for many days, with no break nor chance of any kind, Chulani wandered on wearily with the Parrot-Pandit always following: until at last the blue hills rose up in the distance, and hour by hour grew nearer, with white clouds floating round their hazy peaks, and always a shimmer of heat-mist rising up between them and the hot sandy plain below.

And soon the trees, first parched and straggling, but soon spreading into tall jungles, came again, and call of bird and hum of insect told of life once more. And Chulani breathed again, for that the weary desert was ended, and he drew nigh to the Nága land. And he strode firmly on, longing for high emprise.

But, as he hastened to scale the soaring crags, the Parrot-Pandit stayed him, knowing things to come. For he knew how the Kanduro had warned the Nága king, and already, far off, he saw the danger that would come.

Therefore he spake again, in human voice, "O, Chulani, now will a swarm of serpents, small but terrible, beset thee, crowding up from every crag as thou dost climb; and shaft and arrow will avail thee naught against their countless hosts, but they shall come hissing from afar, hasting in dread array, with poisoned fangs of death and pain."

And Chulani was sad, and said, "If they be so many wherewith shall I slay them? for I am but one, and my quiver will fail."

But the sage Parrot answered, "It is not with weapon that thou shouldst meet them. Thou must bide here, fasting, three days, without fail or fear, and I will fly hence to the land of Damba-diva, where are the seven peaks of Meru, even to the magic tree which the three daughters of Midnight planted; and always with watch and ward they guard it well. But to me will they give of its leaves, and thou shalt anoint thyself with them, and eat of its fruit, and the poison of the serpent-hosts shall be harmless to thee, and every snake that bites through the magic juice of those leaves shall himself die miserably, but thou shalt go on thy way in safety."

So the Parrot-Pandit left him, and flew swiftly on towards the narrow sea that separated Lanka from Damba-diva, seeking the magic leaves. But Chulani was left alone, pondering much on the things which were happening.

And the days passed wearily in lonesome thought, with always the same sky, and same arch of trees, and same stillness brooding monotonously over him. And the second day went, and the third, and fourth and still the Parrot-Pandit came not; till Chulani's heart throbbed restlessly, chafing at delay.

And on the fifth day, as the evening rose slowly up the dim east, with one pale star watching the wan green day that died in the western sky, where the peak of Smanella-kanda loomed gray and dark against the fading light, while the trees waved heavy arms over him wearily, he lay watching the calm still moon rising in her peaceful beauty over the lulled silence, and he fashioned to himself in eager longing the rare loveliness of Amara-dévi shaping forth from the yellow disc in the opal sky; and as he lay, waking-dreaming, sleep came upon him, and he dreamed that down the long-slanting moonbeams came the spirit form of the bright Moon-Meaden, till she stood over him, white and holy, and smiled upon him, her worshipper.

And he lay a little happy while gazing upon the glorious vision and then he murmured, "Ah fairest Queen, why must I tarry so long ere I behold indeed thine own most radiant self, and win thee for mine own?"

But she, soft smiling, made answer, "Why shouldest thou tarry? Why not press on and dare the Nága-sentinel, and wrest the Wishful Jewel? O weary one of little courage, why is thy heart so faint?"

And he awoke, and swore a great oath that naught should stay him more, but in very sooth, come what might, he would be up and doing with the morning.

But he knew not that it was not Amara-dévi at all, but the youngest Kandura who had come to him in his vision. For she had been sent forth by the Nàga king to lure him on, and had taken upon herself the form of Amara-dévi, coming in false beauty down the wan moon-path.

Therefore he rose up at early dawn sorely angered at himself, chiding himself for a fool and a woman for fearing the Parrot-Pandit's tales—what were they, true or false? Was not she, his Queen, awaiting him? And who was he that he should stay?

And he strode off wrathfully, and began climbing the rugged steeps, where the bare rocks jutted out black and sharp from tangled shroud of fern and thorn, steep after steep rising sheer and beetling over him.

And the noonday sun struck hard and hot, and he paused a while for utter weariness, and leaned up against a great rock that cast its grateful shade over the burning slope. But in a moment from among the pleasant grass there sprang a small green snake, and bit him in the hand, and the poison rushed burning through his veins, throbbing and shooting in painful surgings.

And even when he bound up the wound, with teeth hard-set for pain and fear of death, there came a troop of snakes, following after that other, and they all sprang at him in fierce savageness, and the air was filled with their hissing.

But Chulani had leaped up on to a ledge of the rock, and with his back firm set against it he covered himself with his shield, and with an arrow held club-wise he warded off the serpent swarm, dealing blow after blow valiantly, and felling and slaying many an one. But the rest still hissed and writhed and reared their poisonous heads against him and venom from the bite which had taken him unawares swelled his arm till he scarce could hold his arrow, and the poison mounted up towards his heart and head till his brain began to reel and mists rose up before his eyes, and he felt that he must of a surety die.

And he thought bitterly of the Parrot-Pandit, and cursed him for tarrying so long, and himself for not waiting till he should bring the magic leaves, and his Fates for that they had cast his lot in evil chance.

And now he heard the whirring swing of heavy wings overhead and looking up with despairing eyes he saw two huge vultures perching on a crag above him, waiting for the end. And he knew that they were the Kundaro, come to see him die; and for very wrath thereat he roused up and smote more savagely with his arrow-shaft at the serpents, and his strength revived for a little while.

For a little while only. And the Kanduro laughed out and spake in human voice, "Thrice fool! why didst thou leave us when we came to thee fair and rare, the Bird-Maidens of the Passing Hour? Were we not beauteous exceedingly, far above mortal beauty, and what wast thou that thou shouldst have none of us? But the Passing Hour is passed, and its beauty hath departed, and life is lost, and we shall see thee die in woeful plight, we the Vultures of the Lost Past!"

But, with failing breath that came hard and thick, he gasped, answering, "False Fiend-Maidens are ye—a little beauty and a long sorrow—but my Amara-dèvi is pure and bright, and for her would I die a thousand deaths, and thrice as hard and painful as this one."

And they laughed, "Aha! the cold Moon-Maiden, who would die for her? But in very sooth thou thyself wilt soon be cold enough in death."

But he spake no other word to them, still smote on wearily at the serpents, thinking only of his Queen, and he had lost her by not waiting for the Parrot-Pandit, and wondering how it could be that this dream had led him wrong.

And now the night had come, and the Moon shone full upon him, and he looked up for one last sight of his Maiden-Queen; and suddenly his eyes were opened and his ears heard, and a still voice down the moon-ways came to him, "Faint not; I have seen all thy sorrow, and all thy folly, and I know all thy love for me. Fight on and persevere! But heed not again false visions of me, for the vision that bade thee hasten on was none of mine, but it was the youngest Kandura, the handmaid of the Nága king. But now call aloud thrice for the Parrot-Pandit, and he shall bring thee help. Only see that thou disobey him not again."

Then did Chulani in penitence call three times on the Parrot; and straightway, swift speeding through the air, he came with willing wings, bearing a precious branch of the magic tree; and full tenderly he laid the leaves on the serpent-wounds, spreading them gently with anxious care.

And immediately Chulani felt his strength revive, and his life come back with full tide of health; and he stood with downcast eyes before the Parrot-Pandit, and said: "Truly, I was a fool, and thrice a fool for my obstinate haste; because thou wast long gone my spirit rebelled against thee, and the false dream came, and I believed a lie rather than thy truth. But now have I seen my fault, and do thou, this once, forgive."

But the Parrot-Pandit, answered: "Thou art but human, and thou hast but erred. But now must thou fast yet again three days, eating naught and drinking naught save only the juice of these three leaves that I give thee, and they shall give thee strength. For on the fourth day thou must go against the Nága-sentinel, and do battle with him alone; but if ever thy need be sore call thrice for me, and straightway I will be with thee; but now I must tarry here, doing the hest of Sèneka."

And this time Chulani fasted patiently, heeding no thought, nor dream, but biding penitent. And on the fourth day he rose up long ere dawn, as the moon sank down through the mists in the west, and he breathed a prayer to the Moon-Maiden to guard him well, and went forth, clenching firmly quiver and shaft.

And at mid-day he came to a place where the butterfly-pilgrims all flew circling upwards, and a great smoke rose up to the sky, and all the trees were scorched and gnarled; and underneath yawned a great depth of cavern, whence the smoke arose, and hideous sounds of roaring and hissing came forth from the black darkness.

And Chulani knew that he was now come to the abode of the Nága-sentinel, and his heart beat high, and his breath came thick, as he peered cautiously through the tree-trunks, wondering what it were best to do.

For he could see no sign of the monster, nor any access; only a great cloud of smoke, and wall of rock, and flames of fire shot forth through the gloom from the cavern's mouth.

And all that day he waited if by any chance he might see the great serpent come forth, for he feared greatly to go into the dimness blindfold; but there was no sight nor portent, only the muffled sound of hidden horror. And at last as the moon rose yet again, and the weird shadows trooped fearfully round him, he went forth desperate, down into the black cave's mouth, to do or die. And he called out in a brave voice, "Come forth, O Nàga monster, and yield to me the Wishful Jewel!"

Then came a flash of lurid flame from the depths beyond, and through clouds of tawny smoke on a wrathful coil of hooded hideousness with seven hissing heads and darting tongues, and glinting glamour of savage eyes, till Chulani felt the blood run cold back to his heart which stood still for a moment and then thumped cruelly into his very mouth.

But small space had he for thought or dread; for the Serpent was upon him with the seven heads darting fearsomely round him, while he strove to cover himself with his good shield, stepping backward till his back pressed against the damp walls of the cavern; and then he smote out his arrows valiantly, through and through the monster's scaly hood, piercing all in vain. For the beast reared always up again each head that drooped, however sorely wounded, and ever came on fresh to the charge, so that Chulani's arm grew weary, and his heart heavy, and he knew not what to do.

Therefore he called thrice for the Parrot-Pandit in his sore distress, and in an instant there was a swift cleaving of the air and the Parrot flew straight at the monster's eyes, till soon each head was reared helplessly, hissing vainly in blinded rage, so that Chulani thrust securely at him, himself unseen. But still he could not slay his foe, but each wound revived the anger and strength of the grim Nága. United the Parrot-Pandit bade him rub the arrowheads in the mound on the cavern-sides, and smite again. And this time the monster reared up once in death pangs and fell down dead, there on the poison-stained rocks at Chulani's feet.

And straightway from the middle head rolled forth the Wishful Jewel, and Chulani seized it in eager gladness, and gazed at its rare loveliness sparkling in treble lustre of noonday suns, and he called out, "Now, Jewel mine, bring me to Amara-dévi, my bright Moon-Queen."

* * *

And by the Restful Lake, in the whispering sedges, among the long lake-ripples, he stood straightway; and the Moon-Maiden wrapped round in white beauties lay sleeping once more amid lotus-canopies of dreams and quietness; while the whist waters wondered wistfully at the vision, and sweet breezes murmured long love-songs around her, and the guardian stars watched over her.

And swift with ardent joy he swam to her side, and laid his lips to hers as she slept, whispering, "At last, my Queen! I have slain the Nága and won the Wishful Jewel, and now my wish is only thee."

And with a long sigh she turned, and her quiet eyes opened slowly and from their deep stillness gazed down into his soul; and no more did she fly from him, but in surrendered trustfulness she confessed to him all her love, and her joy-thoughts throbbed in phosphorous gleams along the quiet waters.

But soon, too soon, the chill breath of far-off dawn came sighing through the lake-side trees, and the Moon-Maiden shivered and the lotus-cups curled sorrowfully over their folded leaves, and she kissed her brave boy-love sadly, lingeringly:

"Farewell, O mortal love; for I must go and wander all day in the dull heavens, far from the Restful Lake and thee, till the quiet Night shall come again, and I with her, to thee, once more. Farewell, O sweet, for all the weary toil of coming day."

And she rose up slowly to climb the pale wan moon-path with tired steps and all unwilling.

But Chulani for strong love could not refrain, but he cried out, "I will never leave thee, O my Queen! Thy way shall be my way, and thy path my path through the long waste of heaven and sky." And he laid hold of her train of light-lustred robes as she arose, and they twain soared up through the gray sky, on through the endless realms of space.

But soon his brain grew dizzy and his eyes dark that they could not see, and his hold slackened, and down through the trackless ways of whirling worlds he fell, falling always through long years of ages, far from his lost Moon-Queen, for ever and for ever.

And the maids of Lanka saw him fall, a falling star through the fading night.

And never again to the Restful Lake did the lorn Moon-Maiden come and never again did she shine with full splendor on the hated earth, save only on one night in every circuit of her journeying—the one night on which she had known mortal love. But at all other times she mourned with veiled face darkly, night after night shrouding her sad pale face more and more as she wandered farther from the land of Lanka;—only when she turned backward in her long world-wander did she lift her shroud by slow degrees to see again the spot where Chulani had wooed and won her dreamful heart.

So in the old-world days the Moon-Maiden fell from her high estate, loving mortal love.

And so it comes that the Tamil maidens say when they see a falling star, "Give me a faithful love, but not unwise." But the story of Chulani and of Amara-dévi the Moon-Queen in her god-days when her light was always full has been long since forgotten by them.

But the falling stars and Chulani fall on still, and the faithful Moon yet mourns, true to her short, sweet love.

"The Greatest Book of the Century"

KRISHNA:

THE LORD OF LOVE

A History of the Universe.

12mo, 550 pages.
Prices: Morocco, Three Dollars.
Cloth, Two Dollars.

Reviews and Opinions:

Brooklyn Daily Eagle:—An exalted philosophy.

New York Daily News:—Sree Krishna, the Lord of Love, is forceful—an extraordinary book.

Chicago Examiner:—Certainly its ethics are of the most exalted type.

Mrs. Ella Wheeler Wilcox:—It is most interesting. I find it most clearly and simply told. . . . It broadens and interests, and so I enjoy your most exhaustive work on Creation.

Henri Pene Du Bois, (New York American):

I thank you with all my heart for your book. It realizes a dream of my teacher Stephane Mallarme, the poet, for it has three super-imposed texts. One is for the passerby, one for the intellectual, another is for the artist. And all are excellent. And each one is to be read twice—once for the ideas that are expressed, the other for the beauty of the phrases.

"The Listener," Boston Evening Transcript:

In the true spirit of his lordly race, unabashed before modern science, claiming indeed to have anticipated modern science at all points, sturdy in the simplicity and strength of the faith of the antique world, with all the power of singleness of belief in a few grand all-embracing principles, he issues warnings like the prophets of the ancient Hebrews.

In this book "Krishna" is to be found the simplest, most straightforward, most logical exposition of the "Ancient Wisdom" concerning the creation of the universe and evolution thereof, of any the "Listener" has happened to see.

The Oriental Review:

The boldness of the author is simply phenomenal. The world has been looking forward to welcome such boldness. It is the boldness of absolute realization of the Central Truth of Creation, a boldness whose force is living love. It is a boldness which will stagger the spirit of the most captious critic into conviction of the wonderfully luminous interpretations, given in the book, of the spiritual and moral laws and forces of life. . . . . Baba Bharati has dealt the final blow to the West's "swelled-head" notions of its own superiority in enlightenment in this the greatest book of the century, in which he has mirrored forth the inner machinery and the workings of the cosmos, for the benefit of the soul-hungry students the world over, in the easiest English imaginable. The book deserves the largest circulation. It cannot fail to interest all classes of readers. The prose-poems which embody the life-story of Krishna in Part II and the "Revelations" are chants of soul-thrilling word-music unequalled in English literature.

Boston Evening Transcript:

The volume is remarkable for the completeness with which it covers the subject, the extent of the information concerning the different points of the philosophy and religion giving it almost the value of an encyclopaedia of the best in Hindoo thought.

Bharati's style is of singular directness, simplicity and clearness, and his work throughout is marked by sanity, lucid thinking, and the high purpose of one who is devoted, with all the ardor of a strong, manly nature, not to himself but to all humanity.—[Extracts from a two-column review.]

American Review of Reviews:

The volume is really a clear history of the origin, nature and evolution of the universe as the Oriental mind perceives it; it is a clear statement of the doctrine of Karma; an exposition of the caste system; a beautiful story of the Oriental Christ, and perhaps the clearest statement ever published of the Hindoo cosmogony. . . . The love of the source of the universe, which in the Hindoo philosophy is Krishna, is the determining force of the universe. It is an extraordinary book—the fascinating exposition of an exalted philosophy.

Bible Review, Cal.:

This book is written in an open, liberal style, free of all technicalities—very different from other Hindu works; it is designed more for the general reader, and contains no obscure phrases, nor does it enter into any of the rationale or drill for the attainment of powers: the great, pervading spirit being that of pure devotion. . . . The main value of this work is to endue the reader with its sweet spirit of love.

The Outlook, New York:

In personnel the Peace Congress was as notable as its doings. The most striking of all delegates was the Hindo monk Baba Bharati in his robe and turban; tall, powerful, strong and acute, severely condemning England for its invasion of Tibet, full of good will to all, and distinctly affirming the divinity of Jesus Christ.